NTIC   OCEAN

BOCA D
CANGREJOS

PUNTA
LAS MARIAS

ISLA VERDE

TORRECILLAS
LAGOON

INTERNATIONAL
AIRPORT

SAN JOSE
LAGOON

LEGEND:

OLD CITY

BEACH FRONT

CENTRAL DISTRICT

SLUMBELT

OLD SUBURBAN

NEW SUBURBAN

INTERSTITIAL

PIEDRAS

SAN JUAN URBAN AREA
ECOLOGICAL DISTRICTS

A Social Science Research Center Study

COLLEGE OF SOCIAL SCIENCES,
UNIVERSITY OF PUERTO RICO

A study of San Juan, Puerto Rico

B
P THE BEDMINSTER PRESS 1964

THE Urban Ambience

THEODORE CAPLOW

SHELDON STRYKER

SAMUEL E. WALLACE

Readers of this book are invited to send their names and addresses to
The Bedminster Press, Vreeland Avenue, Totowa, New Jersey, U. S. A
to receive announcements and literature about other books in the social
sciences published by The Bedminster Press.

To HARRIET, ALYCE, *and* SONDRA
with affectionate respect

ACKNOWLEDGMENTS

We are greatly indebted to:

Dr. Millard Hansen, Director of the Social Science Research Center of the University of Puerto Rico, for his unfailing encouragement and support of this project.

Our intelligent, competent, and hard-working field staff: Elia Hidalgo, research associate; Vidalina Rodríguez, Livia Paniagua, Delma Ivette Vázquez Arjona, Harold Toro, Ernesto Maldonado, and Arlene Cohen, research assistants; and Carmen Herenia López and Conchita Torruellas Correa of the office staff of the Research Center.

The public officials who graciously provided the basic ecological information about San Juan: Ismael Torres Macías, Subsecretario, Departamento de Obras Públicas; Victor M. Labiosa, Jefe, División de Investigaciones sobre Carreteras, Departamento de Obras Públicas; Laura Martinó, División de Inquilinato, Administración de Estabilización Económica; Rafael Ramírez, Director, División de Energía Eléctrica, Autoridad de Fuentes Fluviales; Rosa L. Stéfani, Departamento de Economía Doméstica, Universidad de Puerto Rico;

Mort Turner, Geological Division, Industrial Laboratory, U. S. Department of the Interior; José Janer, Negociado de Registro Demográfico y Estadísticas, Departamento de Salud Pública; Salvador Capestany, Director, Negociado de Urbanismo; Filiberto García, Director, Negociado de Permisos; Ramón García Santiago, Presidente, Junta de Planificación; Katy Hernández, Unidad de Nóminas de Asistencia Pública, Departamento de Salud Pública; Félix Mejías, Presidente, Autoridad Metropolitana de Autobuses; Rafael Nieves, Decennial Operations Division, U. S. Bureau of the Census; Herminio Sotomayor, Negociado de Tasación Científica; Conrad Taeuber, Assistant Director, U. S. Bureau of the Census.

Pedro A. Jiménez, Subadministrador; Edna Ranck, Directora, Oficina de Investigaciones; Josefina Monseratte, Directora, Servicios Administrativos; Eduardo Figueroa, Diseñador, Oficina de Planificación; and Carlos M. Alvarado, Director Ejecutivo, Administración y Corporación de Renovación Urbana y Vivienda.

Angel Luis Rivera Cedeño, CRUV Office of Administration, spent many days wandering through the city with one of the authors to take the photographs for this publication. The photograph of the New Suburbs was obtained through the courtesy of the Planning Board.

Special acknowledgments are due to Helga Umpierre whose competence and untiring effort made the administration of this project a pleasure and to Ann Sheer and Violeta Mitinas for their painstaking patience with an awkward manuscript.

T. C.
S. S.
S. E. W.

February, 1964

CONTENTS

Introduction

The first sociological study of a neighborhood that we have been able to discover was Thomas Jesse Jones', *Sociology of a New York City Block*.[1] Nearly sixty years have passed since its publication and it has been followed by about forty empirical studies of urban neighborhoods in the United States and elsewhere.[2] Almost all of these describe intensive and mean-

[1] Thomas Jesse Jones, *The Sociology of a New York City Block*, New York, Columbia University Press, 1904.
[2] Among the more important of these are: Roderick D. McKenzie, *The Neighborhood: A Study of Columbus, Ohio*, Chicago, The University of Chicago Press, 1923.

Jesse Bernard, "An Instrument for the Measurement of Neighborhoods with Experimental Applications," *South Western Social Science Quarterly*, September 1937.

The series of studies by Paul Chaumbard de Lauwe under the general title of *L'Agglomeration Parisienne*.

Ruth Hill Useem, John Useem and Duane L. Gibson, "The Function of Neighboring for the Middle-Class Male," *Human Organization*, Vol. 19, Summer 1960.

ingful interaction in the urban neighborhood. Yet one still hears the classic opinion that:

"Neighbors, signifying intimate association, have been replaced by nigh-dwellers, this designating adjacent residences coupled with anonymity." [3]

It was Robert E. Park whose view of urban life as lonely, impersonal and confused,[4] has colored the viewpoint of American urban sociologists ever since. Louis Wirth's classic paper on Urbanism as a Way of Life[5] identified the *disappearance* of the neighborhood as one of the distinctive features of urbanism together with the substitution of secondary for primary contacts, the weakening of bonds of kinship, the declining social significance of the family, and the undermining of traditional bases of social solidarity. The city planner who draws upon this intellectual tradition for guidance in predicting the human consequences of large-scale architectural design, is encouraged to disapprove of the urban environment even as he works with it.

There are many other influences in the heritage of modern city planning that are hostile to cities as we know them[6] and that seek to reverse the normal characteristics of urban life by planning, substituting symmetry for variety, homogeneity of land use for heterogeneity and residential dispersion for concentration.

A number of eloquent critics have recently expressed un-

---

[3] Wilbur C. Hallenbeck, *American Urban Communities*, New York, Harper and Bros., 1951, pp. 536-537.

Not all urban sociologists suffer from this blind spot. A lucid discussion of the "intensity of neighborhood relations" can be found for example in Gist and Halbert's standard textbook, *Urban Society*, New York, Crowell, various editions.

Phillip Fellin and Eugene Litwak have recently proposed a new view of the question. See their "Neighborhood cohesion under conditions of mobility," *American Sociological Review*, Vol. 28, June 1963 p. 76.

[4] Robert E. Park, "The Concept of Social Distance," *Sociology and Social Research*, Vol. 8, July-August 1924.

[5] Louis Wirth, "Urbanism as a Way of Life," *American Journal of Sociology*, Vol. 44, July 1938.

[6] The anti-urban tradition in the United States literally goes back to the Founding Fathers. It is excellently documented in a recent publication by Morton and Lucia White, *The Intellectual Versus the City: from Thomas Jefferson to Frank Lloyd Wright*, Cambridge, Harvard University Press and the MIT Press, 1962.

easiness about the assumptions *behind* master plans and challenged them with empirical data.[7] The revival of argument on questions that had been taken as settled points up the paucity of our knowledge about the social fabric of great cities and suggests that the social consequences of city planning need to be examined more closely, more often, and in more places.

The evaluation of urbanism as a way of life is especially crucial for cities in transition, those compelled to make present decisions about the whole course of their future development. San Juan is of particular interest because of the way it has grown by migration. Most of its new residents come directly from agricultural villages or isolated farms, without intervening stages. Because of its relationship to the United States, San Juan has more industries, more automobiles, more modernity of every kind than would ordinarily be expected in the capital city of an underdeveloped area.

It is also a major *source* of migration. About one in four, of its inhabitants departs in any given year for the United States, the overwhelming majority to the Island of Manhattan.[8] About 150,000 Puerto Rican families maintain a foothold both in greater New York and greater San Juan, with individual members moving back and forth according to the seasons, the vicissitudes of the labor market, or for personal and family reasons.[9]

As if the culture shock of migration from mountain villages to the crowded pavements of San Juan and the interchange of people and ideas with the mainland were not enough, public policy and economic evolution are additional agents of change. Substandard housing is removed and new housing constructed at a dizzying rate. Highway development, industrial development, urban renewal, harbor improvements and the breakneck growth of public facilities displace thousands of families within the metropolitan area

---

[7] The most notable of these critiques is Jane Jacobs, *The Death and Life of Great American Cities*, New York, Random House, 1961.

See also The Editors of Fortune, *The Exploding Metropolis*, New York, Doubleday, 1958.

[8] The contrast between the Island of Manhattan and the Island of Puerto Rico is the subject of a lively and factual musical argument in Act II of Leonard Bernstein's "West Side Story."

[9] See: *Characteristics of the Passengers who Traveled by Air Between Puerto Rico and the United States, October to December, 1961*, San Juan, Bureau of Labor Statistics, 1962.

every year. The stage is thus set to examine rootlessness, anomie, and the consequences of mobility under what seem to be extreme conditions.

One primary purpose of this study is to provide the planners of San Juan with more accurate knowledge of how ecological zones and neighborhoods are structured in their community and how residential conditions can be improved.

But our interest goes somewhat further than the dilemmas of local planning in San Juan. The neighborhood—as it will be described and discussed in this book—is the first stage of society beyond the individual household. The analysis of such miniature social systems may be informative, as a step towards the analysis of larger chunks of social reality that can not be so easily observed or understood.

Thus our inquiry into the San Juan neighborhood will carry us into some reflections on the nature of urbanism and the general question of how small voluntary groups develop and survive. We shall examine such problems as whether an increase in the *intimacy* of associations in a group can be expected to decrease the *number* of relationships and whether people who seek a closer relationship with their social superiors will necessarily avoid the company of their inferiors. Finally, since some of these problems have not been posed in this form before, it will be our continuous effort to find simple forms of expression, either numerical or graphical, for networks of neighboring relationships.

The findings of the study are presented in the following pages in descending order of territorial size. The report starts with a general description of the urban area and proceeds to examine it under progressively higher magnification, so to speak. The first chapter deals with the characteristics of the city, its ecological history, and its relationship to Spanish and North American models. The second chapter examines the ecological zones of the urban area in some detail and the third chapter discusses the barrios into which the city is conventionally divided and then introduces the neighborhoods that constitute the principal sample. The appendix to chapter three provides a good deal of information about these neighborhoods by means of photographs, impressionistic observations, and charts of their interaction networks. The four succeeding chapters are devoted to the analysis of several types of neighborhood data: the correlates of interaction, the relationship between intensity and extensity of neighboring, the basis on which neighbors choose each other for interaction, and the conditions that determine residential satisfaction and stability.

The final chapter discusses the application of these findings to the current problems of city planning in San Juan.

1 The San Juan Urban Area

Some General Characteristics

The Urban Area of San Juan includes the three formerly distinct communities of Old San Juan, Santurce, and Rio Piedras. Together, they comprise the urban core of the San Juan Metropolitan Area, which had more than 600,000 inhabitants in 1962. In addition to the three core communities, the Metropolitan Area includes the five municipalities of Cataño, Bayamón, Guaynabo, Trujillo Alto, and Carolina. These have been excluded from the present study, which is concerned exclusively with the San Juan Urban Area.

Density is the key word for both the island and the city. Puerto Rico is twelve times more densely populated than the United States, five times as crowded as Cuba, and more than thirty times as crowded as the average South American country. The urban core contains a scant 18,000 acres, occupied by more than 300,000 people—an average of about sixteen per acre. This density is achieved despite the fact that the great majority of structures are single family dwellings, and that about a fourth of the land inside the urban perimeter is undeveloped.

Land use is frequently intensive. Seven of the fifty-eight barrios have population densities exceeding one hundred persons per acre. One of them reaches 206 persons per acre. In these districts, a few houses have small interior patios but practically none have yards. The structures approach the limits of each property line, side by side, close to the sidewalk. This architecture, given the necessity for ventilation in a tropical climate, allows the urban family little privacy. The predominant visual impression of San Juan is that of "people, people, everywhere."

While land use has been intensive since initial settlement, San Juan's population growth was not explosive until 1930. The depression years brought thousands of families to the city to overcrowd San Juan and Santurce, and to begin the expansion of Rio Piedras. The end of World War II brought another surge in population growth. Rio Piedras more than doubled in size, and the entire urban area increased by two-thirds. During recent years, San Juan's growth has slowed down considerably. Some of the older districts actually lost population from 1950 to 1960 while suburban expansion increased Rio Piedras by seventy-five percent. The urban area as a whole grew at a modest two percent per year.

TABLE 1

Percent Population Change San Juan-Santurce, Rio Piedras, San Juan Urban Area, San Juan Metropolitan Area, and Puerto Rico, 1930 to 1960.

	1930-40	1940-50	1950-60
San Juan—Santurce	47.5	32.8	−10.9
Rio Piedras	74.9	161.0	75.3
San Juan Urban Area	53.1	62.4	21.0
San Juan Metropolitan Area	42.4	36.2	30.0
Puerto Rico	21.1	18.3	6.3

Source: Bureau of Economics and Statistics, Puerto Rico Planning Board

The figures on population growth do not adequately reflect the extent of the changes taking place. Vast public and private programs must also be considered. Renovation of the urban area has displaced nearly a tenth of its inhabitants.

Highway construction, urban renewal, hotel development, and slum clearance have been responsible for the relocation of about fifty thousand families in the past decade. A single project in Santurce, now in its initial stages, will displace about twenty-five thousand more.

The growth of the building industry suggests the magnitude of change experienced by San Juaneros. Between 1951 and 1961 the annual value of new private dwellings added to the housing inventory increased from twenty-nine million to eighty-two million dollars. The current annual rate of construction is 7600 units, with a base of approximately 100,000 existing units.

The outstanding event in the island's recent history has been the startling increase of money income. Prior to World War II, Puerto Rico was an area of desperate poverty. Twenty years later, stimulated by public subsidy and private initiative, it was regarded throughout the world as a model for the successful development of underdeveloped areas.[1] Per capita income in Puerto Rico today is approximately $700, less than a third as high as in the United States but more than twice the Latin American average. The rapidity of this improvement is not easy to grasp. In 1941, only three percent of Puerto Rican families had incomes of $1,000 or more. Eleven years later (1952) this sector had expanded to forty-three percent. Eight years after that (1960) it reached eighty-nine percent. To put it another way; more than half of all Puerto Rican families had incomes *under* $300 in 1941; within two decades more than half had incomes *over* $3,000.

The combination of decelerating urban growth and rapidly rising economic capacity has partly transformed San Juan from a city of slums to a city of suburbs.

The dual character of this city as part of the American economy and as the capital of an underdeveloped area produces a number of statistical and cultural incongruities. The occupational distribution of San Juan is nearly identical with the urban average in the United States. The only important differences are the much greater number of private household workers and the lesser number of skilled craftsmen in San Juan. By contrast, the literacy and schooling of the ur-

---

[1] For a history of this development see "Aspects of Business and Economic Growth," Chapter III in Thomas C. Cochran, *The Puerto Rican Businessman: A Study in Cultural Change*, Philadelphia, University of Pennsylvania Press, 1959.

ban population still show colonial traces. The average (median) adult left school before completing the eighth grade. The corresponding urban dweller in the United States nearly completed high school. However, equalization proceeds apace. The percent of Puerto Rico's school age population enrolled in school in 1960 (84.7%) was nearly as high as in the United States.

Many demographic features reflect the disappearing colonial identity. San Juan has a much younger population than any North American city. Half of its inhabitants were twenty-one or younger in 1960 compared to about a third of urban dwellers in the United States. Only fifty-nine percent of the adult male population were married in 1960 compared to seventy-one percent of the comparable population on the mainland.

The people of San Juan also vary from the American norm in color, height and weight. These differences, too, are likely to be modified by economic progress, but more slowly.

". . . it is apparent that Puerto Ricans are small-dimensioned compared to the population of the United States. This is best seen in the average weight and stature of the males, with mean values of less than 130 pounds and 5 feet 5 inches; these values are approximately 25 pounds and 4 inches under those for United States male 'separatees' measured following World War II. In their other dimensions the Puerto Ricans, like most Latin Americans are small and gracile. The 'smallness' typical of this population is partly owing to undernourishment and partly to the public health affecting island life, plus a heritage derived from Caucasians who are typically small." [2]

The proportion of non-whites in San Juan was found to be 20.3 percent by the 1950 census[3] compared to 10.1 percent for the urban areas of the United States. The figure for Puerto Rico is biologically and sociologically meaningless, while the figure for the United States is biologically meaningless, but sociologically explicit. The population of San Juan consists "predominantly of Negro and Caucasian elements, with a small mixture of American Indian." [4] All that can be said with certainty is that a very large proportion of Puerto Ricans are visually distinguishable from the run of

[2] Frederick P. Thieme, *The Puerto Rican Population: A Study in Human Biology*, Museum of Anthropology, University of Michigan, No. 13, 1959, p. 65.
[3] Questions regarding color were not included in the 1960 Census of Puerto Rico.
[4] *Ibid.*, p. 44.

the white population in the United States and nearly as large a proportion are also distinguishable from the Negro population.

Gathering Descriptive Data

Even the smallest of modern communities, James West noted in *Plainville*,[5] accumulate too many historical documents for any single reader to review. San Juan is a large community and its structure is so complex that even a review of its principal social characteristics—such as the age, income, literacy, color, or mobility of its population—requires recourse to many different sources of varying reliability.

In order to delineate the ecology[6] of San Juan, data indicating the historical and current distribution of population were needed. While Puerto Rico is filled with official forms and questionnaires, annual statistical yearbooks and coding and tabulating equipment, the researcher soon realizes that some of this quantification is in the manner of Kafka. Enter an office of statistics. The machines are clicking away and everyone seems busy. You take a copy of their annual report (every office has one—though most may be published several years late) and hurry back to your desk. Your examination of the report is soon interrupted by a few unexplained symbols. You return to the office of statistics. The superintendent knows nothing of these details. He refers you to his assistant. The assistant refers you to another, and the procedure is repeated until you reach the clerk who coded the original data. She innocently explains that she thought it best to code the forms by her horoscope. Since no one instructed her differently, and no one checked her work, you find you have been working with her horoscope.

In one office a clerk was assigned to handle all crime reports involving minors. When another office sent her an arrest report, she was to match the two forms and tabulate the

---

[5] James West (pseud.) *Plainville, U.S.A.*, Columbia University Press, New York, 1945.
[6] For a current summary of the theory of urban ecology, see James M. Beshers, *Urban Social Structure*, The Free Press of Glencoe, 1962.

number of delinquents. She decided to simplify matters by waiting for the arrest report. Meanwhile, the clerk in charge of the arrest report decided to wait until she received the crime report before classifying the minors. After a sudden "decrease" in juvenile delinquency was recorded, an outside investigator discovered its cause.

In the traffic bureau, clerks routinely record traffic counts, plot them on maps, and file them away while planners cry for traffic data. In another section, the researcher finds that the ability to speak, read, and write English is ascertained by asking the subject, "Puede usted hablar, leer y escribir Inglés?"

Research assistants are sent out to collect "unofficial" facts like mobility or land values from an agency's files. They begin at a likely starting point (usually a government office). It almost invariably turns out to be the wrong starting point. Thence by persistence they trace a path from one office to another until the facts are located. These are not likely to be found in immediately useable form.

Here, for example, was our routine sampling procedure to obtain mobility data from the files of the Water Resources Authority.[7]

"The meter file is arranged alphabetically and continuously by street names. The entire file is divided into 14 safes which contain 240 drawers each having a capacity of 100 cards. Half of each safe contains cards in the meter file, the other half contains the permanent family record cards. There are approximately 2,000 drawers in the meter file. The purpose of drawing this sample was to compute the average rate of residential mobility per barrio. For convenience of sampling, it was decided to count the 50th in the first drawer and then to select each 50th card thereafter until the 2,000 drawers were exhausted. The work was demanding and uninspiring, the space of the regular staff was limited, tempers occasionally ran high but the Puerto Rican faith in social research prevailed and some simplification was achieved by measuring off the sampling intervals with a ruler. It was necessary to oversample by nearly 20% to compensate for families living outside the defined project limits. All business and industries were excluded. Only two items of information were taken from each meter card —the address and the number of families having utility service from March 1955 to March 1959. Any unit not occupied in March 1955 was excluded, any unit continuously occupied from 1955 to 1959 was counted only once."

Procedures like this were evolved for each of thirty-one indexes in each of twenty public offices. These ranged from

[7] Autoridad de Fuentes Fluviales.

the Archives of the old city of San Juan to the Traffic Bureau and from the Carnegie Library to the Real Estate Board.[8]

Each series constituted a separate problem. In all, data were accumulated on the following characteristics of the San Juan Metropolitan Area: age, school enrollment, income, percentage colored, population change, population density, migration in and out, sex ratio, welfare load, distribution of children, distribution of disability, distribution of private and public school facilities, location of churches, businesses, cemeteries, police stations, post offices, urban concentration, traffic concentration, land use categories, land value gradients, delinquency, mobility, births, deaths, divorces, rental values, non-native residents, bi-lingualism, health indices, age of buildings, and the distribution of soils. These series form the basis for the following description of San Juan.

San Juan, as all observers note, represents a combination of Spanish colonial and modern North American traits. Before describing its growth, it may be well to glance briefly at the typical ecological patterns associated with these two influences.[9]

---

[8] Other agencies were—by their English designations—the Department of Public Health, Puerto Rican Planning Board, Department of Education, Public Welfare Office, Bureau of the Census, Power Authority, Industrial Test Laboratories, Department of the Interior, Family Welfare Association, University Libraries, Home Economics Extension Division, Public Works Department, Treasury Tax Division, Police Department, Department of Commerce, Water Resources Authority.

[9] The published material on the ecology of North American cities is too extensive for detailed citation. A recent collection representing the literature is: George A. Theodorson, *Studies in Human Ecology*, Evanston, Illinois, Row, Peterson, 1961.

The recent improvement in housing statistics in United States metropolitan areas is profitably exploited in such works as Beverly Duncan and Philip M. Hauser, *Housing a Metropolis*, The Free Press of Glencoe, 1960 and Nelson N. Foote et al., *Housing Choices and Housing Constraints*, New York, McGraw Hill, 1960.

The structure of a number of Latin American cities has been studied in some detail; see for example:

A. T. Hansen, "The Ecology of a Latin American City," Chapter 8 of *Race and Culture Contacts*, edited by E. B. Reuter, New York, McGraw Hill, 1934.

Norman Hayner, "Mexico City: Its Growth and Configuration," *American Journal of Sociology*, Vol. 50, January 1945; "Criminogenic Zones in Mexico City," *American Sociological Review*, Vol. 11, August 1946.

Harry B. and Audrey E. Hawthorne, "The Shape of the City: Some Observations on Sucre, Bolivia," *Sociology and Social Research*, Vol. 23, November-December 1948.

Theodore Caplow, "The Social Ecology of Guatemala City," *Social*

The Spanish Colonial City[10]

City planning was well developed when Hispanic colonization began. The master plan for city founding and development was laid out in the "Laws of the Indies." [11] The ante-
cedents of this plan are found principally in the works of
Eximenic.[12]

Writing in the second half of the fourteenth century, Eximenic began by proposing a rectangular street pattern. He
argued that this pattern was preferable not for its practical
value nor ease of defense but for its beauty.

A city should be geographically located for easy growth but
should always be surrounded by four walls. Each of these
walls should contain a guarded entrance in its center. Each
entrance would be connected with the opposite wall by an
avenue. Thus, the city would have two major avenues of
transportation, dividing it into quarters.[13]

Each quarter has its own small market-place,[14] friar's home,
and the commercial shops necessary for daily living. Each
quarter is further sub-divided into parishes, inhabited by persons in the same or similar occupations. The location of each

---

Forces, Vol. XXVIII, December 1949 and, The Modern Latin American
City, Vol. II, Proceedings of the 29th International Congress of Ameri-
canists, University of Chicago Press, 1952.

Dan Stanislawski, "The Anatomy of Eleven Towns in Michoacan,"
Latin American Studies, No. 10, University of Texas Press, 1950.

Marvin Harris, Town and Country in Brazil, New York, Columbia
University Press, 1956.

Richard M. Morse, From Community to Metropolis: A Biography of
São Paulo, Brazil, Gainesville, University of Florida Press, 1958.

Lucila Herrmann, "Estudo ecológico de uma radial em São Paulo,"
Boletim da Associacao dos Geografós Brasileiros, São Paulo, Vol. 2,
March 1942.

[10] Since Spanish influence was predominant in the initial planning and
early growth of the urban area, our discussion is focused on the Spanish
colonial city of the sixteenth century.

[11] See Appendix to Chapter One.

[12] For a thorough discussion of Eximenic and his works, see Leopoldo
Torres-Balbas, Resumen Historico del Urbanismo en España, Madrid,
Graficas Uquina, 1954, pp. 90-107.

[13] Ibid., p. 91.

[14] Plaza del Mercado.

occupational group is determined by convenience to place of work. For example, farmers are located near the wall facing the country, sailors near the sea, and merchants near the market. In general, this implies that the social status of the population should decline from the center to the periphery, with slums outside the city walls.

A large central market plaza is placed at the axis of the two main roads. It is constructed to allow traffic to circulate around it, without interfering with the people congregated within. This central plaza serves the social and economic needs of the entire urban population. The cathedral is on the central plaza with the Bishop's palace and the cemetery adjoining. All other buildings surrounding the plaza are of uniform architecture and height, lower than the cathedral, to enhance the cathedral's magnificence.

The Royal Palace, Eximenic continued, should be located on one side of the city, next to the walls, with an outside entrance. The hospital, leper colony, gambling houses, and brothels should be placed on the side opposite the prevailing wind.

Eximenic's proposals were made more than a century before they were adopted in the Indies. By then, some features of Eximenic's plan were already part of the typical urban configuration in Spain.

Originally, the cathedral with an adjoining cemetery occupied the center of small Spanish cities.[15] In addition to its primary function, the cemetery also served as a market and meeting place. The pressure of population increase, however, soon shifted both the cemetery and the market outside the city walls—this time in different locations.[16]

As the market expanded, some temporary buildings were constructed for the merchants and their goods outside the city walls. These buildings gradually developed into slums,[17] which grew along the periphery of the market. More respectable residential dwellings followed, until the city walls were expanded; then the market-plaza again occupied a central location in the city.

Thus, at the beginning of the sixteenth century, the market plaza was the social, economic, and geographical center of the city.[18] It functioned as a meeting place, a theater, an

---

[15] Torres, *op. cit.*, p. 83.

[16] *Ibid.*, p. 85.

[17] *Arrabales de mercadores.*

[18] Richard Robert, "La Plaza Mayor en España y en America Española, *Estudios Geográficos*, Madrid, Vol. 11, No. 39, May 1950.

area for public meetings and announcements, for religious and secular programs, for bull fights, games, and finally as a market.

The cathedral, all municipal buildings, and the homes of the wealthy, surrounded the central market-plaza. The neighborhoods of the city were composed of homogeneous social classes, with the slums either next to the walls or outside them. This was the urban configuration predominant in Spain, and the one visualized in the "Laws of the Indies," when the city of San Juan was founded.[19]

The North American City[20]

In the ecologist's conception, city expansion takes place through the processes of concentration, centralization, segregation, invasion and succession. Concentration takes place at natural barriers which create a "break in transportation"—a place where goods must be transferred from one type of transport to another.[21] Centralization occurs around this employment-providing site. Competition for land determines land values which in turn segregates commercial, industrial, and residential establishments according to their ability to pay land costs.

In the processes of invasion and succession, the composition (symbiotic balance) of an area is upset by incoming migration. The former residents move out, enabling more migrants to move into the district, until they occupy the major portion of it (succession). The out-migrants move

[19] The city's location and main features were planned and some attempt was made to follow the plan in other details.
[20] The discussion follows the original model of city growth first presented by Robert E. Park and Ernest W. Burgess in The City, Chicago, University of Chicago Press, 1924.

For later theoretical treatments see: Amos H. Hawley, Human Ecology, New York, Ronald Press, 1950; Edgar M. Hoover and Raymond Vernon, Anatomy of a Metropolis, Cambridge, Harvard University Press, 1959. Beverly Duncan, Georges Sabagh and Maurice D. Van Arsdol Jr. "Patterns of city growth," American Journal of Sociology, Vol. 67, January 1962.
[21] For example, from ocean going vessels to land transport.

into an adjacent area to start the same process there. The overall effect is to create several successive rings of growth, called zones, similar to those formed on water when a pebble is dropped into it. There are five roughly concentric and somewhat homogeneous zones.

The first zone, usually the geographical center of the city, is the central business district. Its size is limited by the range of pedestrian traffic—about a mile or less. The commercial and service units within the districts are clustered by type, creating specialized areas for banks, theaters, restaurants, night clubs, department stores, and other facilities.

Zone two, the zone of transition, contains a hodgepodge of urban functions—rooming houses, markets, skid rows, transportation terminals, light industry, and the cultural enclaves of recent immigrants. Since absorption into the central business district is anticipated, this area shows more structural deterioration than any other.

The third zone may be characterized as lower income residential. In the usual case, it was built up before the advent of zoning, and includes a mixture of commercial, industrial, and service facilities.

Zone four consists largely of owner occupied single family dwellings, built under strict zoning. Non-residential establishments are confined to spaced intersections. Although this zone is homogeneous in its residential land use, it contains a mixture of socio-economic strata.

The outermost circle, the urban fringe, is larger than all others combined and its outer boundaries are not well defined. It includes new residential developments, private estates, semi-rural villages and farms, heavy industry, golf courses, cemeteries, airports, and a variety of other facilities that require extensive space.

An Ecological History of San Juan

San Juan city was established in 1521 as part of the Spanish empire's program to retain supremacy in the Caribbean. The site was selected primarily on military considerations. In choosing to fortify the tip of the small peninsula which overlooks the harbor, the Spaniards sought to assure control of the harbor of San Juan which meant effective control of the island.[22]

The selection of this particular site and its intended function had several important results in the city's later growth. The centralization of political functions in San Juan, plus the military protection available nowhere else, secured a politically dominant position for the city from its initial founding to the early part of the twentieth century.

San Juan city was also located at a "break in transportation"—a place where goods had to be transferred from ocean going vessels to land transport. This impetus to rapid growth, so favorable for many cities, failed to exercise a significant influence on San Juan until 1825, or somewhat later, due to Spanish trade policies. Spain prohibited coastwise shipping from other parts of Puerto Rico to San Juan city, in order to prevent smuggling. Since the island's topography made overland routes extremely difficult, local commerce did not flow to or from San Juan in its early history although it was the only port where ships could legitimately land.[23] The "break in transportation" at San Juan had little influence on the city until the 19th century when roads were improved and some coastwise shipping was allowed. These trade policies inadvertently but effectively isolated San Juan city from the rest of the island and its rural inhabitants.

The military character of the city had other important consequences. There was a real and continuous danger of attack from the time of initial settlement through 1800. The first fortifications were begun only ten years after colonization of

---

[22] Arturo Morales Carrión, *Puerto Rico and the Non Hispanic Caribbean: A Study in the Decline of Spanish Exclusivism*, Rio Piedras: University of Puerto Rico Press, 1952, pp. 4-5.
[23] *Ibid.*

the island, and by 1641, the city was completely walled.[24]

The colonial government, whose employees constituted a large segment of the city's population, was supported by annual grants from the Mexican treasury. Owing its existence to the government and to the garrison, the city grew very slowly. Nevertheless, even with a low annual average increase, the small space enclosed by the city walls was sufficiently overcrowded to require expansion by 1650.

Expansion could not take place directly outside the city walls, for the military authorities feared the protection that buildings near the walls would offer an enemy. When San Juan city reached its saturation point, fragmentation of the community by the founding of new settlements was necessary, since expansion of the old city walls remained administratively impossible.

The site of the first new settlement, called Rio Piedras and established in 1714, was determined by considerations of transportation and topography, and by the desire for maximum protection without fortifications.[25] The distance from San Juan city to Rio Piedras represented a day's haul by the available means of transportation at that time. The absence of marshes and an easy overland route (now Avenida Ponce de Leon) were important factors also. Finally, its distance from the coast offered some protection against attack from the sea.

Prior to the settlement of Rio Piedras, some houses had been built in the section known as Santurce. Although this settlement was closer to San Juan, it was exposed to easy attack on two sides, and could be isolated from both San Juan city and the interior. Few were enthusiastic about such a location and its development lagged behind that of Rio Piedras.

Both San Juan city and Rio Piedras were laid out according to the "Laws of the Indies," while Santurce never had the benefit of any city plan.[26] The growth of the urban area from

[24] Puerto Rico Coast Guard Artillery Command, A History of the Harbor Defenses of San Juan, Puerto Rico, Under Spain, 1509-1898. San Juan: Antilles Coast Guard Command, 1944, pp. 17-20.

[25] Adolfo de Hostos, Ciudad Murada: Ensayo del Proceso de la Civilizacion en la Ciudad Española de San Juan Bautista de Puerto Rico, Havana, Editorial Lex, 1943, pp. 65-73.

[26] Puerto Rico Planning Board, A City is People, Commonwealth of Puerto Rico, Office of the Governor, San Juan, Puerto Rico, 1954. This useful little publication presents historical maps showing the settlement pattern of the present metropolitan area for 1508, 1521, 1550, 1650, 1750, 1800, 1850, 1900, 1940, and 1950.

its founding until 1900 was relatively slow, and spatial adjustments took place in the planned communities of San Juan and Rio Piedras without any serious difficulty. This did not occur in Santurce, because of the lack of plan, and some difference in function. Santurce seems to have been an interstitial, somewhat formless area between San Juan and Rio Piedras. It was never an autonomous community, but developed as an uneven ribbon, along the road from San Juan city to Rio Piedras.[27]

The rate of population growth in the urban area increased sharply after 1900. The three major communities grew quite differently.

San Juan city reached its peak in 1920 and subsequently began a decline which continued uninterrupted through 1960. While San Juan had only doubled its population in the 50 year period 1900-1950, the population of Santurce in 1940 was four times its total for 1900. Rio Piedras did not experience rapid growth until 1940. Ten years later, in 1950, its population had more than doubled. It nearly doubled again from 1950 to 1960.

Thus the current urban configuration proceeded from Spanish settlement on the tip of the peninsula, restrictions on the growth of the original settlement, fragmentation into a second settlement, development of an intermediate area between the two, decline of the first settlement as the population shifted to the intermediate area, partial displacement of the city center, and the blurring of old boundaries in the course of growth.

The Unnucleated City

Great cities may be usefully classified as *nucleated*,[28] *polynucleated*, or *unnucleated* and as either *crescive* or *planned*—although there are some mixed and intermediate situations.[29] The nucleated city, like Chicago or London, is tightly

[27] *Ibid.*
[28] The term was first introduced by R. D. McKenzie.
[29] The best summary of alternatives in urban structure, covering a very wide historical and geographical range is Jean Comhaire and Werner

concentrated around a single center and the land use at any point can only be understood when orientation to the center is taken into account.[30] The polynucleated city, like Peking or Algiers, consists of separate quarters or districts, each of which has its own center and its own ecological pattern.

San Juan, like a few cities in the United States whose principal growth occurred in the Age of the Automobile, seems to represent a new type of unnucleated city. It is a rather good example. Other cities of the same general type, like Los Angeles, exhibit a vestigial pattern of nucleation.

All large cities are essentially intersections at a junction of routes. But for purely strategic reasons, Old San Juan was removed from its original inland location of Caparra and placed at the tip of a peninsula[31] where it commanded the harbor but was isolated from the island's road network. As trade and traffic increased in the nineteenth century, a sizeable cluster of population and services developed around the plaza of Rio Piedras, some eleven miles to the southeast and the closest main junction of North-South and East-West roads.

The old city of San Juan was surrounded by exceptionally heavy fortifications which did not quite outlive their usefulness until the very end of the Spanish occupation. Photographs taken just before the Spanish-American War show volunteer groups of citizens helping to knock breaches in the walls while their ladies served refreshments.[32] There were no important changes in the street plan of Old San Juan from 1650 to 1900 and not many more to this day. Even when the walls were breached, the possibilities of peripheral expansion were severely limited by the sea to the north, the fortress of El Morro to the west, and the harbor to the south. On the eastern side was a narrow sandy isthmus, most of which was already occupied by military and harbor installations. The displacement of the land intersection and the lack

---

J. Cahnman, *How Cities Grew: The Historical Sociology of Cities*, Madison, New Jersey, The Florham Park Press, 1959. See also Kevin Lynch, "The Pattern of the Metropolis" in Lloyd Rodwin (ed.), *The Future Metropolis*, New York, George Braziller, 1961.

[30] Nucleated cities often come in pairs like Minneapolis and St. Paul, Buda and Pesth. Such pairs are always of unequal size and the smaller member of each pair is likely to have a less definite pattern.

[31] Until recent times the peninsula was really an island and the mainland was reached by ferry across an arm of the harbor.

[32] *San Juan Star*, Tuesday, February 16, 1960.

of expansion room around the old city help to account for the curious fact that after 1900 most of the population growth occurred *between* San Juan and Rio Piedras in a ribbon development along both sides of the main road (Avenida Ponce de Leon).

In time, the ribbon widened and filled all the space between the harbor and marshes on one side, the sea front and the lagoon on the other.

By 1950 the northern part of the area was completely settled and the tide of settlement had washed up to each of its natural boundaries. About that time, the open spaces surrounding Rio Piedras began to be claimed by "picture-window" subdivisions and these are still being built, moving southward and westward and even further away from Old San Juan.

In a nucleated city, the transport of goods and persons is minimized by the concentration of traffic facilities like offices, stores, factories, terminals, warehouses and markets in a small central area, and the segregation of related facilities (the theater district or the financial community) in even smaller areas, so that internal transportation involves short distances.

In a nucleated pattern the daily commuting streams— movements of workers, students, shoppers, and recreation seekers—flow in and out from the periphery to the center along well-defined channels of mass transportation. Land values are highest in the central district, where the concentration of people and facilities is heaviest, and land prices decline towards the periphery in proportion to the distance. The use to which land at any point in the urban pattern will be put depends upon the ability of alternative functions to bear the ground rent, and there is an inherent tendency for similar functions to be grouped together in rather homogeneous districts. The modern practice of zoning greatly accentuates this tendency.

The desirability of any area for residential purposes, being influenced by the land value mechanism and the growth of distinctive districts, is theoretically a function of its distance from the center. For example, upper class residential districts develop at the very edge of the central business district where access to the facilities of the central city is at a maximum, but also far out on the periphery where the low price of land permits a lavish allocation of space for the individual dwelling.

The automobile makes the unnucleated city technically

possible by freeing homes and work places from a fixed and expensive transportation network. It would be virtually impossible to design a system of public transit to meet the present transportation requirements of the San Juan population. Automobiles provide access to all parts of the city for the whole population, even without nucleation.

In the unnucleated city, there is very little reason for a store or factory or government office to be in one place rather than another. Land values are moderate throughout the commercial and industrial areas, location is not predetermined by ecology. Workshops, palaces and hovels are likely to be found on the same street. The tavern, the tannery and the seminary keep cheerful company. People are not easily characterized by where they live. A street address carries no status ascription.

The basic pattern of greater San Juan conforms to this description, but it is modified, so far as housing is concerned, by two factors—the irregularity of the terrain and a complicated zoning system. There are few cities in the world whose districts vary so much in climate and desirability. It is only a few minutes walk from the Condado beachfront, perpetually cooled by the sea breeze, to the insect-ridden swampy shores of the San José Lagoon.

There is no discernible relationship between the quality of a residential district in greater San Juan and its proximity to a central district. Those sites most favored by nature—along the beach and on high ground—show the highest land values. Naturally disfavored sites, especially along "dead water," are occupied by slums.

Neutral sites, without conspicuous advantages or disadvantages, like most of Santurce, have heterogeneous residential populations.

Zoning works no fundamental change in this pattern, but serves to abate certain nuisances (like keeping the tanneries away from the seminaries) and to encourage speculation. For example, only a few sites on the beach are zoned for multiple dwellings. In the face of an enormous demand for such facilities, land values there have been rising at a North American rate.

The economic and social disadvantages of the unnucleated pattern are evident. Vehicular and pedestrian traffic is generated out of all proportion to the size of the community. All establishments suffer the common handicap of inconvenient location with respect to the other establishments with which they must maintain contact.

In the case of San Juan, the problem is accentuated by topographical limitations. There are only two main streets running the length of the metropolitan area and the corridor through which they pass is too narrow to permit the development of additional routes without prohibitive cost.

Unlike the traffic pattern of a nucleated city, which shows very heavy peaks during morning and afternoon commuting hours, and secondary peaks at the beginning and end of the evening, San Juan traffic is heavy throughout the working day and light during the evening and night hours. The traffic jam along the main arteries of Santurce is chronic and continuous in the daytime. In addition to commuting (including considerable lunch-hour commuting) the dispersion of facilities generates enormous traffic during working hours. The daily volume of recorded vehicular traffic over the Martin Peña bridges was 79,000 vehicles in 1959. The significance of this figure can best be appreciated if we remember that the entire island of Puerto Rico had 90,000 vehicles registered in that year.[33]

The disadvantages of the unnucleated plan are fairly obvious. Such central facilities as museums, theaters, department stores, libraries, parks, hospitals, and even markets, tend to be underdeveloped in proportion to the size of the community. This dispersion of functions and people seems to hinder communication on all levels of activity and to be partly responsible for the duplication of effort which sometimes seems to be characteristic of Puerto Rico.

The advantages of the unnucleated plan are not so evident but they can be inferred from some of our information about residential mobility and neighborhood satisfaction. The era of explosive growth in San Juan has been succeeded by an era of intensive rebuilding. Public housing projects and vast suburbs of tiny single-family houses are rapidly replacing the slums and squatters' shacks of the past. Meanwhile, the rich grow slightly richer and much more numerous, the tourist trade increases its demand for semi-permanent semi-luxurious housing and a steady supply of construction credit encourages expansion of upper income housing, too. Between these extremes, the dwellers in the mixed and heterogeneous neighborhoods in the central ribbon of settlement from Old San Juan to Rio Piedras show a fairly high level of satisfaction with their housing and neighborhood

[33] Commonwealth of Puerto Rico, Bureau of Traffic, Department of Public Works, *Traffic on the Main Arteries of the San Juan Metropolitan Area*, 1959.

facilities. It has been possible to shift large segments of the population from crowded shacks in the older districts to un-crowded, plain concrete houses in the new subdivisions. Some of these, lost among the sand hills, look terrifyingly bleak to the outside observer but we have no basis on which to deny the obvious contentment of their inhabitants.

APPENDIX

City Planning in the Laws of the Indies

(Archivo Nacional, Madrid, Ms. 3017 Bulas y Cedulas para el Gobierno de las Indias)

San Lorenzo, July 3, 1573.
I the King
Ordinances for discoveries, new settlements and pacifications.

110. . . . . After having made the discovery and selected the province, district and land to be peopled and the sites where new settlements are to be founded those who intend to settle are to proceed in the following manner:

On arriving at the locality where the new settlement is to be founded (which according to our will and ordinance must be one which is vacant and can be occupied without doing harm to the Indians and natives or with their free consent) the plan of the place, with its squares, streets, and building lots is to be outlined by means of measuring by cord and ruler, beginning with the main square from which streets are to run to the gates and principal roads and leaving sufficient open space so that even if the town grows it can always spread in a symmetrical manner. Having thus laid out the chosen site the settlement is to be founded in the following form.

111. The chosen site shall be on an elevation; healthful; with means of fortification; fertile and with plenty of land for farming and pasturage; fuel and timber; fresh water, a native population, commodiousness; resources and of convenient access and egress. It shall be open to the north wind. If on the coast care is to be taken that the sea does not lie to the south or west of the harbor. If possible the port is not to be near lagoons or marshes in which poisonous animals and corruption of air and water breed.

112. In the case of a sea-coast town the main plaza which is to be the starting point for the building of the town, is to be situated near the landing place of the port. In inland towns the main plaza should be in the centre of the town and of an oblong shape, its length being equal to at least one and a half times its width, as this proportion is the best for festivals in which horses are used and any other celebrations which have to be held.

113. The size of the plaza shall be in proportion to the number of residents, heed being given to the fact that towns of Indians, being new are bound to grow and it is intended that they shall do so. Therefore the plaza is to be planned with reference to the possible growth of the town. It shall not be smaller than two hundred feet wide and three hundred feet long nor larger than eight hundred feet long and three hundred feet wide. A well proportionated medium size plaza is one six hundred feet long and four hundred feet wide.

114. From the plaza the four principal streets are to diverge, one from the middle of each of its sides and two streets are to meet at each of its corners. The four corners of the plaza are to face the four points of the compass, because thus the streets diverging from the plaza will not be directly exposed to the four principal winds, which would cause much inconvenience.

115. The whole plaza and the four main streets diverging from it shall have arcades, for these are a great convenience for those who resort thither for trade. The eight streets which run into the plaza at its four corners are to do so freely without being obstructed by the arcades of the plaza. These arcades are to end at the corners in such a way that the sidewalks of the streets can evenly join those of the plaza.

116. In cold climates the streets shall be wide; in hot climates narrow, however, for purposes of defense and where horses are kept the streets had better be wide.

117. The other streets laid out consecutively around the plaza are to be so planned that even if the town should increase considerably in size it would meet with no obstruction which might disfigure what had already been built or be a detriment to the defense or convenience of the town.

118. At certain distances in the town smaller, well proportioned plazas are to be laid out on which the main church, the parish church or monastery shall be built so that the teaching of religious doctrine may be evenly distributed.

119. If the town lies on the coast its main church shall be so situated that it may be visible from the landing place and so built that its structure may serve as means of defense for the port itself.

120. After the plaza and streets have been laid out building lots are to be designated, in the first place, for the erection of the main church, the parish church or monastery and these are to occupy respectively an entire block so that no other structure can be built next to them excepting such as contribute to their commodiousness or beauty.

121. Immediately afterwards the place and site are to be assigned for the Royal and Town Council House, the Custom-House and Arsenal which is to be close to the church and port so that in case of necessity one can protect the other. The hospital for the poor and sick of non contagious diseases shall be built next to the church forming its cloister.

122. The lots and sites for slaughter houses, fisheries, tanneries, and such like productive of garbage shall be so situated that the latter can be easily disposed of.

123. It would be of great advantage if inland towns, at a distance from ports were built on the banks of a navigable river, in which case an endeavor should be made to build on the northern river bank, all occupations producing garbage being relegated to the river bank or sea situated below the town.

124. In inland towns the church is not to be on the plaza but at a distance from it in a situation where it can stand by itself, separate from other buildings so that it can be seen from all sides. It can thus be made more beautiful and it will inspire more respect. It would be built on high ground so that in order to reach its entrance people will have to ascend a flight of steps. Near-by and between it and the main plaza the Royal Council and Town House and the Custom-house are to be erected in order to increase its impressiveness but without obstructing it in any way. The hospital of the poor who are ill with non contagious diseases shall be built facing the north and so planned that it will enjoy a southern exposure.

125. The same plan shall be carried out in any inland settlements where there are no rivers, much care being taken that they enjoy other conveniences requisite and necessary.

126. No building lots surrounding the main plaza are to be given to

private individuals for these are to be reserved for the church, Royal and Town house, also shops and dwellings for the merchants, which are to be the first erected. For the erection of the public buildings the settlers shall contribute and for this purpose a moderate tax shall be imposed on all merchandise.

127. The remaining building lots shall be distributed by lottery to those of the settlers who are entitled to build around the main plaza. Those left over are to be held for us to grant to settlers who may come later or to dispose of at our pleasure. In order that entries of these assignments be better made a plan of the town is always to be made in advance.

128. After the plan of the town and the distribution of the lots have been made each settler is to set up his tent on his lot if he has one, for which purpose the captains shall persuade them to carry tents with them. Those who own none are to build huts of such materials as are available, wherever they can be collected. All settlers, with greatest possible haste, are to erect jointly some kind of palisade or dig a ditch around the main plaza so that the Indians cannot do them harm.

129. A common shall be assigned to each town, of adequate size so that even though it should grow greatly there would always be sufficient space for its inhabitants to find recreation and for cattle to pasture without encroaching upon private property.

130. Adjoining the common there shall be assigned pastures for team oxen, for horses, for cattle destined for slaughter and for the regular number of cattle which according to law, the settlers are obliged to have, so that they can be employed for public purposes by the council. The remainder of land is to be sub-divided into as many plots for cultivation as there are town lots and the settlers are to draw lots for these. Should there be any land which can be irrigated it is to be distributed to the first settlers in the same proportion and drawn for by lottery. What remains over is to be reserved for us so that we can make grants to those who may settle later.

131. As soon as plots for cultivation have been distributed the settlers shall immediately plant all the seeds that they have brought or are obtainable, for which reason it is advisable that all go well provided. All cattle transported thither by the settlers or collected, are to be taken to the pasture lands so that they can begin at once to breed and multiply.

132. Having sown their seeds and provided accommodation for their cattle in such quantities and with such diligence that they can reasonably hope for an abundance of food, the settlers, with great care and activity are to erect their houses, with solid foundations and walls for which purpose they shall go provided with moulds or planks for making adobes and all other tools for building quickly and at little cost.

133. The building lots and the structures erected thereon are to be so situated that in the living rooms one can enjoy air from the south and from the north, which are the best. All town homes are to be so planned that they can serve as a defense or fortress against those who might attempt to create disturbances or occupy the town. Each house is to be so constructed that horses and household animals can be kept therein, the courtyards and stockyards being as large as possible to insure health and cleanliness.

134. Settlers are to endeavor, as far as possible, to make all structures uniform, for the sake of the beauty of the town.

135. The faithful executors and architects and persons who may be

deputized by the governor for the purpose shall be most scrupulous in carrying out the above instructions and in hurrying both field labor and house building so that the town may be completed in a short time.

136. If the natives should wish to oppose the establishment of a settlement they are to be given to understand that the settlers desire to build a town there not in order to deprive them of their property but for the purpose of being on friendly terms with them; of teaching them to live in a civilized way; of teaching them to know God and His Law by means of which they shall be saved. This shall be explained to them by the friars and clergy and persons deputized by the governor, by means of good interpreters. Attempts are to be made by all fair means to establish the settlement peaceably and with the consent of the natives. If, after many different attempts have been made to gain their consent the natives still withhold it then the settlers are to proceed to establish their town but are not to take any of the personal belongings of the Indians or to do them more hurt than what may be necessary in order to protect the settlers and enable them to build without interference.

137. While the new town is being built the settlers, as far as possible, shall try to avoid communication and intercourse with the Indians and are not to go to their villages or amuse themselves or disperse themselves over the country. Nor are the Indians to enter the circuit of the settlement until the latter is complete and in condition for defense and the houses built, so that when the Indians see them they will be filled with wonder and will realize that the Spaniards are settling there permanently and not temporarily. They will consequently fear the Spaniards so much that they will not dare to offend them and will respect them and desire their friendship. When the settlers begin to construct the town the governor is to appoint some one to take charge of the sowing and cultivating of wheat and vegetables so that the settlers can immediately employ these for their maintenance. The cattle are to graze and be tended in a safe place where they can do no injury to the cultivated lands or anything else belonging to the Indians. The aforesaid cattle and their offspring are to be at the service of the settlers and for their use and subsistence. . . .

Translated by Zelia Nuttall,
Hispanic American Historical Review,
Vol. 5, 1922, pp. 249-254.

2 The Six Ecological Zones

Barrios and Zones

We are accustomed to a neat convergence of ecological characteristics in nucleated cities of the North American type. For example, in the transitional zone surrounding the central business district, we expect to find a moderately young population of mixed ethnic origin, high residential mobility, irregular family composition, a high incidence of crime, delinquency, alcoholism, schizophrenia, and dependency, associated with high land values, low dwelling rents, high population density, and a pattern of mixed land use.

It remains to be seen whether the character of districts is less distinct in an unnucleated city. At first glance, the San Juan Urban Area presents a chaotic picture. The distribution of architectural and social characteristics seems to be almost random. Statistical characteristics, like land value or the age of the population, are not geometrically distributed with reference to a central point. Indeed, it is impossible to identify the central point of the metropolitan complex.

Nevertheless, we began with the assumption that there *is* an orderly pattern of some kind. This chapter reports the successful search for a zonal pattern, describes the zones and their distinctive styles of life, and presents some of the statistical indicators that enable us to draw zonal boundaries.

The search starts with the smaller territorial unit called the barrio.[1] The San Juan Urban Area is divided into 58 barrios. The term *barrio* has a meaning similar to the French *quartier*. It is something between an autonomous district and a census tract. In some of the old Spanish city plans, the central district—the city proper, with its cathedral and government buildings—was surrounded by barrios at each point of the compass. Each barrio was a miniature city with its parish church and government building on its own small plaza.

By ancient convention, the barrio is a socially recognized community, almost a city within a city. It is not an administrative subdivision and there is no requirement that all barrios have similar areas or populations. This interesting circumstance haunts the sleep of the ecological investigator in Latin America. In San Juan, for example, barrio populations in 1960 ranged from 376 to 60,959!

The surface area varied from Pozo del Hato with a ragged twelve *cuerdas*[2] to Gobernador Piñero with almost three thousand. Nor is there any consistent relationship of population and area. Some of the largest barrios are densely populated; some of the smallest are almost deserted. Certain barrios, like Las Casas, are almost nations in themselves, having a local dialect and an aversion to strangers. Others are so vaguely bounded that many of their own inhabitants cannot identify them.

To make matters worse, the barrios in the old parts of the city are traditional in name and identity, but their boundaries have been changed several times. A few barrios have been eliminated altogether by slum clearance or harbor improvement.

The barrio boundaries once settled (or at least compromised) it remains to take data—like the information from the water meter cards—which are arranged by street

[1] Census tracts were devised and used for the first time in the 1960 census.
[2] One cuerda = .97 acres.

address and distribute each case to the appropriate barrio. This operation involves curious problems.

The Puerto Rican attitude towards addresses is distinctive. Dwellings are often located by reference to the stop numbers of the street car lines—which disappeared many years ago. An informant will give his address as "around the corner from stop 23" without further elaboration. The experienced resident knows where stop 23 *used to be* when the trolleys ran. Houses lack numbers in many of the older districts. There are even streets without names. Letters reach their destinations with the help of an efficient grapevine.

In the newer suburbs, there are too *many* numbers, and the same street name may appear half a dozen times at widely separated points. To add to the confusion, it is a local custom to change street names without notice.

The limitations of these data are evident. It might have been possible for us to devise a more accurate and uniform system for sub-dividing the metropolitan area, but had we done so, none of the available information would have been referable to a population base. It might also have been possible to use the new census tracts, but only at the cost of discarding all information about trends. The defects of the barrio classification, especially their variation in area and population, must be accepted in order for us to be able to say that delinquency or color television or some other index of disorganization has a frequency of X per thousand of the population, and that this varies meaningfully from one part of the city to another.

There is a startling amount of diversity in San Juan. It has a longer history than most American cities. More than four centuries have passed since its foundation. Its culture is hybrid, containing a thorough mixture of Hispanic and North American traits. The range of wealth is unusually great, from poverty just this side of starvation to fantastic affluence. The rate of change is high. Whether we view the city as an architectural design or as a social network, its shape may be seen to change from month to month, under the impact of migration, slum clearance, a housing boom, highway development, the continued expansion of tourist facilities, and the rapid progress of industrialization.

It is pleasing, and a little surprising, to discover a definite zonal pattern in this confusion. By this we mean that it is possible to group the barrios of the San Juan Urban Area into territorial units composed of contiguous barrios with similar statistical characteristics and similar styles of life. It might be more accurate to say that they group themselves, since recognition of the six zones emerged from the study of maps showing the distribution of demographic, economic, structural and social characteristics among the barrios.

The pattern differs in three important respects from what we would expect to encounter in a North American city. First, there is no central business district. For reasons already noted, the facilities that belong in a central business district are widely scattered in this city. Second, there are no regular gradients from one zone to the next. In the classic North American model of concentric zones, many characteristics such as land value or sex ratio show a gradient of regularly increasing or regularly declining values from the center to the periphery. This is not the case in San Juan, although there begins to be some gradation of land values from the beach towards the interior. Third, while most North American cities can be visualized as variations on the same general plan, San Juan appears to be unique, in the sense that its zonal pattern must be explained in terms of its particular history. So far as we can tell, it does not closely resemble other metropolitan communities in Latin America (like Mexico City or São Paulo) that have also expanded from a colonial nucleus.[3]

By way of compensation, the zonal pattern in San Juan is exceptionally clear-cut and highlights the problems of local planning:

The six ecological zones are:

1. The Old City—including all the barrios within the walls of San Juan Antiguo.
2. The Beach Front—consisting of the five barrios fronting on the ocean and Condado Lagoon between Puente Dos Hermanos and Isla Verde.
3. The Central District—composed of the Santurce barrios on both sides of Avenida Ponce de Leon.
4. The Slum Belt—a chain of eight barrios set in low marshy land along dead water for the length of the Martin Peña canal and a little further.

[3] For the ecology of Mexico City, see Norman S. Hayner, "Mexico City: Its Growth and Configuration," *American Journal of Sociology*, Vol. 50, January, 1945, and "Criminogenic Zones in Mexico City," *American Sociological Review*; V. II, August 1956; for São Paulo, see Richard M. Morse, *From Community to Metropolis: A Biography of São Paulo, Brazil*, Gainesville, University of Florida Press, 1958, and L. Herrmann, "Estudo ecológico de uma radial em São Paulo," *Boletim da Associacao dos Geographós Brasileiros*, São Paulo, Vol. 2, March 1942.

5. The Old Suburbs—the six large barrios in the west and north of Rio Piedras.
6. The New Suburbs—the five large barrios in the south and east of Rio Piedras.

A few of the barrios in the urban area have been omitted from the zonal classification. El Morro, the army base, Isla Grande, the naval base, and Hoare, a former slum almost entirely cleared, are considered non-residential. Puerta de Tierra, between the Old City and the Central District, and Shanghai, between the Beach Front and the Slum Belt, are interstitial in character.

A seventh zone, not included in this study, would be the Outer Strip, extending from Bayamon to Carolina. It is counted as part of the metropolis for planning purposes but not as part of the urban area. Its communities are still detached and partly autonomous, although heavily influenced by the onrushing expansion of the New Suburbs.

The Old City

San Juan Antiguo, La muy leal y noble ciudad de San Juan Bautista, the old walled colonial town commanding the entrance to the rich port of San Juan,[4] is still quite intact. It follows the lines of its old walls of which substantial sections are standing. The street plan has not changed in nearly three centuries, although most of the streets have been renamed. The plan is a surprisingly regular gridiron, less than ten blocks long in either direction, bounded by the semi-oval of the old fortifications to the east, an ancient suburb on the little peninsula of La Puntilla to the south, the old viceregal palace with its grounds and water gate to the southwest, the military post of Fort Brooke tipped by the great walls and towers of El Morro to the northwest, the ocean to the north, and the grounds of the old fortress of San Cristóbal to the northeast. The neck of the peninsula, maintained as a clear field of fire in Spanish times, is now occupied by official

[4] In the sixteenth century the island was San Juan and the town Puerto Rico. The semantic shift by which the names were reversed is not unusual in the history of islands.

buildings, port facilities, and at its eastern end, a cluster of parks, hotels and beach clubs, all interspersed with scattered light industry, automobile dealerships and public housing.

The Old City has two main plazas. The Plaza de Colón at the site of its main landward gate, is now the principal bus terminus for the metropolitan area. The Plaza Baldorioty, formerly the Plaza de Armas, is a somewhat unusual version of the traditional central plaza. One side is occupied by the Alcaldía, still used as the city hall. The center is laid out as a park for formal promenading with a bandstand and statues. It contains neither of the city's two cathedrals, which occupy small plazas of their own nearby. The predominant character of Plaza Baldorioty is commercial. It is bordered by two large department stores, and a number of shops and vending stands.

Small as it is, the Old City still shows traces of its ancient division into quarters, with official life in the vicinity of La Fortaleza, shipping activities concentrated in the southeast quadrant, commercial development in a band between the two plazas and residential occupancy along the northern edge.

This part of San Juan has considerable architectural homogeneity. The oldest buildings go back to the original foundation and have been almost continuously remodeled. Most of the newer buildings date from the early years of the twentieth century. They are colonial in basic plan, but with heavy Victorian touches. Unlike some other Latin American capitals, San Juan has not suffered from earthquakes. Some of the seventeenth century buildings in the Old City are three, four and five stories high. In most of the residential streets towards the sea, the predominant design is an unbroken row of one story houses with gates and grilled windows opening directly on the sidewalk.

One of the world's most spectacular slums, La Perla, rises on the steps of a natural amphitheater facing the sea not far outside the walls. Within the Old City, there are no slums. Public services are fully available, if somewhat old-fashioned. The buildings, with very few exceptions, are solidly constructed, although sometimes sub-divided beyond reason. A large scale restoration is now gathering momentum, with the intention of enhancing the colonial atmosphere.

The Old City has shown a loss of population in every decennial census since 1920 and there has been a steady exodus of commercial and governmental activity in the same period. This is curious, considering that it was fully occupied

then and is fully occupied now. What seems to have occurred is a decline in density, still imperceptible in the
crowded streets and plazas.

The residential population is a cross-section of the social
pyramid, but an old-fashioned cross-section, with the poor
very numerous and the rich very rich. There are startling
contrasts from one block to the next in the northern quarter.
In some neighborhoods, the street scene includes naked
children at play, gossiping women in the doorways, circles of
old men seated on the sidewalks, the blare of radios and
televisions, the honking of blocked vehicles, the cries of street
vendors, and fights in the local *Cafetines*. Other neighborhoods nearby are almost identical in the façades they present
to the street but shuttered, deserted, with no passers-by, except now and then a uniformed maid on an errand, and no
noise except the mutter of a passing sports car.

The Beach Front

If the naval base at its western tip is excluded, Santurce is
roughly rectangular in shape. The rectangle is bounded on
the north by the ocean, on the south and east by the Martin
Peña Canal and San Jose Lagoon, and on the west by the
harbor. The northern edge of this rectangle is the Beach
Front district. On the southern and eastern edge, following
the "dead water" lies the Slum Belt. The district between is
a hodgepodge of urban functions.

The beach itself is magnificent, a wide strip of sand slop-
ing gently into the surf, with a few large rocks, its line curv-
ing just sufficiently to provide a view of both land and sea
from every point. It has been carefully protected from non-
residential use and except for a few small strips, from private
enclosure. There is no bordering road for most of its length.
The narrowly spaced residential streets end at the edge of
the sand.

Throughout Latin America, the change from the enclosed
city of the past to the suburbanized city of the present was
marked at a fairly early stage by the migration of the rich
from their large old patio-centered houses near the plaza to

landscaped villas in a park-like district outside the traditional limits. This has been the pattern in Mexico City and Guatemala City, in Havana and Montevideo, in Rio de Janeiro and Cartagena. It is virtually universal. In the case of San Juan the location of this suburban settlement was preordained. When the outward migration of upper-class families began early in this century, the open land closest to the Old City and in every way the most desirable for suburban settlement was the magnificent beach along the north edge of Santurce. It had stood almost unoccupied for four centuries, the soil too sandy for vegetable gardens, the beaches offering no shelter for fishing boats, the level terrain giving no protection from hurricanes. None of these disadvantages counted for suburban settlers whose houses would be built to resist storms, whose gardens would thrive on imported top soil and for whom the beach was to be a playground.

After the villas came the related institutions of luxurious living: clubs, restaurants, private schools, hospitals and hotels.

Given the income distribution that prevailed in the 1920's, when the principal settlement of the Beach Front occurred, there was enough room in this zone to accommodate all of the families interested in suburban settlement. Increasingly, the upper income families who first occupied these barrios were joined by middle income families seeking the same style of life on a more limited scale.

The most eventful change in recent years has been the development of tourism. The first major hotel, the Condado Beach, was completed in 1921, and sufficed for a long time to accommodate a small number of winter tourists and a larger number of business and official visitors, and to provide room for the receptions, formal dinners and other public festivities of the moneyed minority. It was not followed by a second hotel until 1948, when the Caribe Hilton was constructed with government assistance. Skeptics doubted that it would ever be filled and even its planners did not venture to predict that it would operate close to full capacity—occasionally above capacity—all through the year. The development of the tourist industry was a remarkable feat of integrated public planning, aided by a brilliant promotional campaign and a number of helpful accidents like the decision of Pablo Casals to settle in San Juan, the availability of bargain air transportation from Idlewild to Isla Verde, the development of resorts in the Virgin Islands, and the shutdown of Cuban tourist facilities after the rise of Castro. The results have followed the general outlines of the official plan but have exceeded all expectations. In the decade of the 1950's, the number of hotel rooms more than tripled. By 1962 there were more than four thousand hotel rooms and more than thirty guest houses at the Beach Front. An additional two thousand rooms were under construction.

At the beginning of this period, this invasion tended to displace the larger estates and the villas with their extensive grounds, while leaving the middle-income beach neighborhoods nearly untouched. The more recent period has seen the wholesale development of condominiums, cooperative skyscraper apartment houses, most of them built very close to the sea. The flight of the upper class families to the more distant suburbs continues while at the same time the ancillary establishments of the tourist trade—coffee shops, night clubs, dress and souvenir shops, auto rental and travel agencies—appear in increasing numbers around the sprouting new hotels.

The Central District

This is a fish-shaped sector with its head in the Condado Lagoon and its tail extending from the Expreso Norte to Avenida Borinquen. It is separated from the ocean by a belt of beach front barrios, from the bay front and the dead water channel by a belt of slums. The Central district is not easy to describe since its hallmark is heterogeneity. About half of the barrios in the urban area are in this zone and as may be seen from the descriptions and photographs in the Appendix to chapter three, there is little similarity among them. Income, residential stability, family composition, occupational distribution and indices of social welfare vary widely and unpredictably from one barrio to the next, and indeed within barrios.

Neither the architectural style nor the arrangement of houses and public spaces show any consistent design. Most of the structures in the Central District were constructed between 1900 and 1940, without benefit of public or private community planning. The usual facing is stucco but there is some use of masonry and brick, and whole streets of wooden houses. There are stores with Moorish and Gothic façades, villas copied after those of the Riviera, ultra-modern mansions designed for indoor living in cold climates, faceless wooden houses with big porches like midwestern boarding houses, streets of little tropical villas and other streets of grimly respectable brick duplexes.

The Central District leaves a prevailing impression of confusion, aside from its heterogeneity. The mixture of functions is extraordinary. Expensive villas nestle between lumberyards. An automobile body shop faces an apartment house. A twelve story steel and glass office building sprouts incongruously from a bed of semi-detached wooden houses. A medical clinic is sandwiched between a warehouse and a driving school.

The residential transitions are even more startling. Around the corner from a lavishly landscaped mansion, newly completed, is a row of run-down tenements and disreputable bars, with a convent school at the corner.

The only uniform characteristic of Santurce is traffic blight. In all its avenues, streets and alleys, traffic is heavy, slow and noisy throughout the daylight hours. Parking is difficult. Pedestrian movement is dangerous. The smell of gasoline is ubiquitous. On the main avenues the traffic jam is continuous. The overflow spills into the side streets, and fills them quickly without alleviating the pressure.

The only important structural features of the Central District are the parallel main thoroughfares of Fernandez Juncos and Ponce de Leon. These emerge almost from the gates of the Old City and run parallel to the Condado Lagoon and diagonally across the Central District to its southern edge where they touch briefly, and then with Fernandez Juncos changing its name, diverge again to run parallel all the way through Rio Piedras. The principal business concentration of the urban area is found along and between these two avenues in the Central District, in a ragged, ribbon development. In the past, this concentration had no center or point of maximum concentration although pedestrian and vehicular traffic was heaviest at stop 22.

The extension of the Expreso Norte, the opening of a new major intersection at stop 18, and the one-way routing of traffic on the main thoroughfares is beginning to change the shape of the central business district. Both vehicular and pedestrian traffic are now concentrated at stop 18 and commercial expansion on both sides of the new cross street has been rapid. Land values have fallen on Ponce de Leon and risen on Fernandez Juncos. They are beginning to peak at stop 18, where the beginnings of a commercial nucleus are visible.

The Slum Belt

The peninsula on which the Old City is built is really an island, connected to Santurce by bridges. Santurce itself is nearly an island, bounded on the north by the sea, on the west by San Juan Bay, on the east by the shallow stagnant San José lagoon. The lagoons are connected to the bay by the Martin Peña Channel. This dead water route has been used for decades as the main sewer of the urban area. The bordering land is low, swampy, and frequently flooded. It has hardly any economic value.

The Slum Belt extends along the northern side of the canal and continues out into the bay at one end and along the banks of the lagoon at the other. There are spots of slum housing on the southern side of the canal also. This strip has been occupied by squatters for at least fifty years but the major growth of the Slum Belt occurred in the thirties, when the depression drove thousands of desperate rural families into the city. Each family would collect any available material—scrap lumber, packing boxes, crates, discarded metal—select a site and build a shack. They would begin with one room and add more space as resources and circumstances permitted.

The first comers selected sites within fairly easy reach of transportation. Later as the barrio became more crowded, newcomers started building their homes immediately behind their neighbors, with access through narrow passageways. When all the better land was occupied, construction continued over swamp and open water. A family would sink piles into the mud for a foundation, finish the house and then build a solid base for it by throwing refuse under the floor. Many of these houses cannot be reached except by a long trail of planks over mud and water. Originally, there were no public services at all, not even police and fire protection. Electricity and running water were not available in the Slum Belt until the past decade. Now the government provides street lighting, health and welfare services, and even builds wooden sidewalks where possible. The removal of the entire Slum Belt is an official planning objective.[5] It is still very far from realization although some of the worst districts have been cleared and their populations relocated.[6]

There is a surprising variety in the style and condition of the Slum Belt houses. Generally, housing quality decreases and overcrowding increases with proximity to water. Differentiation also results from the history and collective experience of each *barriada* (small barrio). These have distinctive names. Some recall a topic of current interest at the time of construction: *Bravos de Boston, Corea, El Ultimo Chance, Tokio.* Others are satirical: *Buenos Aires, Buena Vista, Vista Alegre.* A few express a state of mind: *Sin Perdida, Hato del Puerco, Fondo del Saco.*

The present slum belt extends continuously for more than five miles along the canal. Eighty-six thousand people live here, with an average density of nearly one hundred persons per acre. Welfare cases, infant mortality, tuberculosis, pneumonia, delinquency, truancy and other indices of social pathology are much higher than anywhere else in the urban area. Income, education, and life expectancy are much lower. Small wonder that many prefer the Isle of Manhattan.

[5] Passage of the 1949 Housing Act marked the beginning of serious relocation in Puerto Rico. In 1950-51, thirteen new projects with 6,056 units and costing $36 million were begun. By 1961, 26,556 units costing $143 million had been completed. An additional 3,256 units were under construction. Even with this greatly expanded program the CRUV (Corporación de Renovación Urbana y Vivienda) estimates that an additional 164,000 units must be built in the next decade, in order to reduce the slum population to only ten percent of the Island's urban population.

The typical project consists of a series of three story buildings. Each building contains eighteen apartments, with some variation in the number of bedrooms. Six families share a common stairway. Rent is adjusted to family income, ranging from three to sixteen dollars monthly.

[6] For a discussion of the human aspects of slum clearance in San Juan, see Kurt Back, *Slums Projects and People*, Social Psychological Problems of Relocation in Puerto Rico, Durham, N.C., Duke University Press, 1962.

The Old Suburbs

South of the Martin Peña Bridge, Avenida Ponce de Leon continues in a straight line to the old center of Rio Piedras, paralleled by its sister thoroughfare which becomes the Avenida Muñoz Rivera after crossing the canal. The three barrios that border these avenues on the east and the two on the west make up the Old Suburbs. Their combined area excluding public land is about equal to Santurce and at first glance this zone rather resembles the Central District. Many of its structures date back to the 1920's and some, especially near the main plaza of Rio Piedras, to the nineteenth century. The presence of a few older buildings, and the rapid deterioration of paint and roofing in buildings built to mediocre standards, tends to conceal the newness of the "old" suburbs. In fact, nearly half of the existing residences have been built since 1955.

The double thoroughfare merges at the Agricultural Experiment Station just south of the old center of Rio Piedras and becomes Commonwealth Highway No. 1 to Caguas. The bordering territory, although recently urbanized, has had a long history of occupation and the growth of the city caught up a number of large installations in its path—the Naval Radio Station, the Quintana Hipódromo, the School of Industrial Arts, the campus of the University of Puerto Rico and the intact center of the provincial town of Rio Piedras, with its public buildings, its park and bandstand, its open air markets, and a distinctive physiognomy.

The two great avenues show no intensive commercial development as they run through the Old Suburbs but are lined with a variety of establishments: automobile lots and garages, discount houses, repair shops, private schools, warehouses, convents, asylums, supermarkets, neighborhood stores, research institutes, shopping centers, office buildings, apartment hotels, banks. Many of these were only recently established. It is clear that the fragmented and unsystematic distribution of commercial and service facilities in the Central District is being extended to the Old Suburbs.

Behind the main streets, most of the streets are exclusively residential. The houses in one neighborhood, although not necessarily identical, usually have a family resemblance. The streets are wide and well-paved. Pedestrian traffic is considerable but there is little animation and family life is lived within four walls rather than on the public stage. Respectability, comfort, social security, shiny cars and upward mobility are the banners that fly over these barrios. Most of the architecture is not recognizably Hispanic. Few of the folkways are tropical. The family of a white collar commuter in the Old Suburbs probably differs less from its Continental counterpart than any other social unit in Puerto Rico.

The New Suburbs

The New Suburbs lie south and east of the Old Suburbs. They were open country only yesterday and the limits of the big new barrios still include farms and villages, woodland and plantation. Most of the urban structures are single family houses, rising overnight on the bare hills in geometrical clusters of hundreds and thousands. There are few schools, or public buildings of any kind, fewer offices or factories, hardly any theaters or shopping centers. The houses have electricity, running water, and septic tanks but no telephones or resident physicians or local churches. Most of the families in these *caserios* do not have their own cars. Their sole linkage to the metropolitan community is by bus and *publico*.[7]

The houses differ somewhat in size and quality but they all reflect a single pattern of single family, one story, picture window "ranch houses," built on concrete block with composition roofs, each standing squarely in the middle of its narrow lot, with a lawn of some kind in front and a yard of some kind in back, identical with its neighbors except for slight variations in color and size. These subdivisions on their treeless hills, under the open sky away from all sight and sound of the city, seem extraordinarily isolated.

One result of this isolation is an amazing variety of makeshift commercial developments. The subdivision resident may wake one morning to find the house next door converted

---

[7] Taxis that carry passengers along fixed routes.

into a barber shop, grocery store, candy store, dress shop, garage, machine shop, music studio, or "professional college for secretarial studies."

Subdivision development began after World War II in substantially the present form but the volume of construction has mounted by leaps and bounds. In the single year of 1960 about 7,000 project houses were constructed. In July 1961, twenty-one subdivisions intended to accommodate 122,000 persons were before the Planning Board for approval. At that time, stricter building controls were introduced to check the excesses of jerry building and profiteering that had inevitably developed.

Population

To the visitor and the tourist, the San Juan urban area consists mainly of the Old City and Beach Front with a fringe of slums in the background and a vaguely defined belt of settlement beyond. The pattern that emerges from census enumerations is quite different. The center of population of the urban complex lies in the Old Suburbs, which have nearly a third of the total population. The Old Suburbs are bordered on the north by the Slum Belt, with more than a sixth of the total, and on the south by the New Suburbs with the same proportion. The population of the New Suburbs alone in 1960 was equal to the combined populations of the Old City, the Beach Front and the Central District and, of course, was increasing much faster.

The 1960 distribution of population represented a considerable change from 1950. In the earlier year, the combined population of the Old City, the Beach Front, and the Central District was three times as large as the New Suburbs and exceeded that of the Old Suburbs. The Slum Belt was relatively much larger than now. Its population was almost three times as large as that of the New Suburbs.

The percentage changes in the single decade 1950 to 1960 explain these startling shifts. The newer parts of the city grew both by taking the lion's share of new migration and by drawing families from the older areas. The population of the

New Suburbs increased by 174 percent, of the Old Suburbs by 43 percent.

The Old City, without any marked change in its buildings, street plan, or visible appearance, lost 31 percent of its population. The Central District lost 21 percent. Only at the two extremes of socio-economic scale was the population relatively stable.

On the Beach Front, the gradual erosion of the wealthiest residential districts by the miscellaneous establishments related to the tourist trade was barely counterbalanced by the development of vacant land and the construction of luxury apartments. The population grew by nine percent. In the Slum Belt, the program of large scale clearance that eliminated entire barrios of slum dwellings during the decade was barely sufficient to offset the natural increase of the slum population and the continued pressure of rural migration. The tide was stemmed but not turned. The Slum Belt population declined by only five percent from 1950 to 1960. In relation to the total urban population, of course, its relative decline was substantial.

Population Density

The foremost characteristic that differentiates the ecological zones is density. The residential population in 1960 showed a density of more than 90 persons per acre in the Slum Belt, 71 in the Old City, 42 in the Central District. There were just over 20 persons per acre on the Beach Front and in the Old Suburbs and half that number in the New Suburbs.

Although the differential between the Slum Belt and the New Suburbs is about nine to one, there is an unmistakable trend towards the equalization of density. Ten years before, the differential between the Slum Belt and the New Suburbs was more than 25 to 1, and in earlier years this difference and the other differences among the ecological zones must have been greater still.

To sum it up another way, the Beach Front and the Slum Belt show fairly constant densities. The nature of land occupancy in both these cases precludes much variation.

The densities of the Old City and the Central District are decreasing very rapidly, however, while the density of the suburbs increases correspondingly. This represents a major departure from the style of life and the architectural configuration that have been characteristic of Spanish colonial cities for three centuries and more. Whether the shift from multiple to single dwellings and from high to low density land use involves disintegration of the neighborhood as a social unit or isolation of the individual family in its separate house, is a question we will consider later in this report.

Residential Mobility

The very rapid changes that are taking place in the distribution of population among the ecological areas of San Juan are not accompanied by as much residential mobility as might be anticipated. More than half of all the dwelling units in the urban area were occupied by only one family during the four year period from March 1955 to March 1959. At the same time, there is surprisingly little variation in residential mobility rates among the ecological areas.

The average number of families occupying each dwelling unit from 1955 to 1959 ranged from 1.5 in the Old City and the New Suburbs to 2.1 in the Central District and the Old Suburbs.

A word of explanation may be useful here. Although it seems paradoxical, there is no necessary correlation between residential mobility and population changes in urban districts. A city with a very high rate of residential mobility may show very little population change in its component districts if most changes of address take place within the same district and most families who move are replaced by other families of similar characteristics.[8] It is conceivable that the distribu-

8 A study of residential mobility in Minneapolis in the period following World War II showed this phenomenon very plainly. Although the metropolitan community was decentralizing at the time, only one out of every sixteen changes of address contributed to the outward movement of population.

Theodore Caplow, "Incidence and Direction of Residential Mobility

tion of a city's population might change rapidly with a *low* rate of residential mobility, if changes of address were normally from one district to another and successive occupants of a dwelling unit usually differed in their social characteristics.

Both of these extreme situations are found in the San Juan urban area. Three out of four families settling at a new address in the Old City come from elsewhere in that zone, most of them from another address in the same barrio. At the other extreme, more than five-sixths of the families moving into a new house in the New Suburbs come from other zones, or from outside the urban area. In attracting migrants from other zones, the New Suburbs have by far the greatest drawing power, followed by the Beach Front and the Central District. Unexpectedly, the Old Suburbs have the least drawing power. Now that they are fully settled they have ceased to attract families from other zones. Most of the residential mobility recorded in the Old Suburbs is a shifting and settling of the population already in place.

The new settlers from outside the city include a very large group of migrants from the rural areas of the island, smaller groups of migrants from other urban areas, returnees from the United States, and a scattering of continentals and foreigners. For this large miscellaneous group the New Suburbs again have the most drawing power, the Old City and the Slum Belt are least attractive. Migrants from the country no longer begin their climb up the residential ladder from an initial foothold in the slums. They are far more likely now to start in one of the larger, less expensive subdivisions in the New Suburbs.

Sex, Age and Color

The number of males per 100 females in the population varies sharply from one zone to another and even from one barrio to another in the older districts. The urban area as a

in a Minneapolis Sample," *Social Forces*, Vol. 27, May 1949. A study of Milwaukee at about the same time showed that most migrants from city to suburb came from the outermost edge of the city's residential area.

Richard Dewey, "Peripheral Expansion in Milwaukee County," *American Journal of Sociology*, Vol. 54, September 1948.

whole shows a sex ratio of 92 and a considerable surplus of females. A low sex ratio appears to be characteristic of urban populations in moderately urbanized countries, especially in Latin America.[9] It is caused primarily by the preponderance of young women among rural-to-urban migrants and is accentuated by an apparent increase in the life expectancy advantage of women under urban conditions. However, in countries of advanced urbanization where most of the inhabitants are city dwellers, the urban sex ratio rises to the neighborhood of 100.

In the case of San Juan, the matter is complicated by the presumably uneven sex ratio of migrants to the mainland, who have never been precisely enumerated.

The Old City is unique among the ecological zones of San Juan in having a large surplus of males. There were 118 males for every 100 females in 1960. The Beach Front has an even greater surplus of females. There were only 74 males for each 100 females in that population in the same year. The Slum Belt, curiously enough, shows the closest approach to equality. The sex ratio there is 98.

The Puerto Rican population is extraordinarily young and the median age of twenty-three for San Juan is more than ten years below the urban average in the United States. The differences among the zones are spectacular, and have remained fairly stable since 1950. The Beach Front has a moderately old population with a median age of thirty-two while the Slum Belt population, with a median age of eighteen is spectacularly young. The other zones fall in between, but both the New and Old Suburbs have surprisingly young populations, considering their economic level.

No emuneration by race or color has been made in Puerto Rico since 1950 and it is unlikely that this characteristic will be taken into official account in future censuses. The 1950 data, by ecological zones, are given for what they are worth but do not show much of current interest. The Beach Front had by far the lowest proportion of non-whites in that year and the New Suburbs, not yet suburbanized, the highest. The Slum Belt stood exactly at the urban average. Segregation by color, although not unknown in San Juan, occurs by blocks or by neighborhoods, not by zones or even barrios. In contrast to the United States, it is much less important than education or income as a stratifying variable.

[9] Kingsley Davis and Ann Casis, "Urbanization in Latin America," *Milbank Memorial Fund Quarterly*, Vol. 24, April 1946 and July 1946. Parts I and II.

Economic Level

As the tables show, there is impressive differentiation among the six zones with respect to income. Median family income in the Beach Front in 1960 was nearly three times as high as the average for the urban area while in the Slum Belt it was only half the same average. The order of descending prosperity is Beach Front, New Suburbs, Old Suburbs, Central District, Old City, and Slum Belt, and the differences are highly significant.

Median family income was not obtained in the previous census, but a comparison of per capita income in 1950 with median family income in 1960 indicates that the differentiation among the ecological zones has increased markedly during the decade, with some change of order as well. The barrios of the New Suburbs were inhabited mainly by poverty stricken farmers in 1950 and the populations of the Old City and the Central District could not yet be described as underprivileged. [Table 11]

Other indicators of economic welfare tell a rather similar story. Median contract rent, for rented dwelling units, ranged in 1960 from $111 on the Beach Front to $49 in the Old Suburbs and $21 in the Slum Belt. [Table 12] The proportion of rental units in the total number of dwellings shows an altogether different distribution. Home ownership is highest in the New Suburbs and the Slum Belt, low in the Central District and very low in the Old City. The Beach Front and the Old Suburbs are almost evenly divided among owning and renting families. [Table 13]

Automobile ownership shows almost the same rank order as income by ecological zones except that the rate for the Old City is even lower than for the Slum Belt. The special character of Puerto Rico as an undeveloped area is nowhere more clearly shown than in these figures. It is altogether remarkable that in the poorest districts of San Juan one in eight families owns a private automobile. In a few especially prosperous barrios the proportion of automobile ownership approaches one hundred percent. [Table 14]

The age of construction is correlated with economic level in a general way. Figures could be obtained in 1959, giving for each zone the percentage of dwelling units constructed during the four years previous. This was low for the three poorer zones—Old City, Slum Belt, and Central District—very high for the Suburbs, fairly low for the Beach Front. [Table 15] The numbers of housing units connected to public sewers reflect peculiarities in the local situation rather than economic indicators. The Old City is highest in the amenity followed closely by the Old Suburbs; the Slum Belt is very low; the remaining zones all show about two out of three homes so connected. [Table 16]

School Attendance

The percent of the school age population enrolled in school rose sharply in every ecological zone from 1950 to 1960. [Table 17] The present rank order is curious: the suburbs show the highest school enrollments, the Old City and Slum Belt are lowest, but the range is only from fifty-four to sixty-eight percent and it is clear that equalization of educational opportunity is proceeding at a very rapid rate indeed.

Public Assistance

There were four kinds of public assistance for which ecological distributions could be secured. These were: welfare aid, old age assistance, disability payments, and aid to dependent children. The figures are surprising in some respects. [Tables 18-21]

The Beach Front has a negligible allocation of public assistance, less than one case per 1,000 of the population in each category. The New Suburbs are second to the Beach Front in each of these distributions with frequencies ranging from four to fourteen per thousand of the population.

The Old City and the Slum Belt are almost equal in welfare aid received (thirty-eight cases per 1000) and old age assistance (fourteen cases per 1000). The Slum Belt, however, has twice as many cases of aid to dependent children as the Old City, apparently due to the much higher proportion of children rather than a greater tendency to claim aid.

In sum, the residents of the Slum Belt appear as unexpectedly moderate claimants on the public funds. The Central District shows the highest rate for old age assistance and the Old City for disability payments.

Delinquency

Juvenile delinquency as recorded by the police is low for the entire urban area, but varies significantly among the six zones, being more than four times as high in the Slum Belt as on the Beach Front. Local knowledge hints that delinquent acts committed by the adolescent members of prosperous families tend to be overlooked, condoned, privately treated or otherwise specially handled and so under-reported. Nevertheless, the official figures do bear a meaningful relationship to delinquency as a public problem.

When delinquent acts are arrayed by place of commission, the distribution is quite different. The suburbs are again low but the Slum Belt shows a favorable rate, while the Beach Front and Central District are highest. Delinquent acts are often committed in the more prosperous barrios by individuals or gangs on forays from the less prosperous. [Table 22]

These figures are for zones. The discrepancy between the distribution of delinquents and of delinquent acts is much more marked when taken by the barrio. The perception of delinquents as invaders from districts where "people live differently than we do" adds a good deal to the threatening character of delinquency and reinforces existing motives for suburbanization. [Table 23]

Traffic Accidents

The table shows the number of traffic accidents reported per standard measure of surface area in each zone in a sample month selected at random. The picture is crystal clear. The Central District specializes in accidents, with a rate three times as high as the Old City, the Beach Front and the Slum Belt. The Old Suburbs are slightly safer than average while the New Suburbs, not directly involved in the traffic snarl, report only negligible casualties. [Table 24]

APPENDIX

*Characteristics of Barrios and Ecological Zones
San Juan Urban Area*

TABLE 1

Population Growth of San Juan[1] and Puerto Rico,[2] 1508-1960

	San Juan (1)	Puerto Rico (2)	% (1)÷(2)
1508	150		
1521	400		
1550	500		
1650	3,000		
1750	9,000	44,883[3]	20.1
1800	11,000	155,426	7.1
1850	25,000	583,308	4.3
1899	34,297	953,243	3.6
1910	51,800	1,118,012	4.6
1920	77,263	1,299,809	5.9
1930	128,121	1,543,913	8.2
1940	189,182	1,869,255	10.1
1950	357,205	2,210,703	16.2
1960	432,377	2,349,544	18.4

[1] 1508-1850 data from *The City is People*; 1899-1960 data from United States Bureau of the Census.
[2] All data from United States Bureau of the Census.
[3] Population for 1765.

TABLE 2

Population Density by Barrios, 1960

	Area 1960 (in cuerdas)	Population	Density (per cuerda)
SAN JUAN ANTIGUO			
El Morro	67.57	387	5.7
San Cristóbal	55.78	3599	64.5
Mercado	26.09	5312	203.6
Catedral	32.36	2285	70.6
Marina	48.55	723	14.8
San Francisco	30.24	1714	56.6
Puerta de Tierra	367.05	8075	21.9
SANTURCE			
Isla Grande	357.57	2319	6.4
Miramar	151.96	4796	31.5
Hoare	84.88	122	1.4
Alto de Cabro	55.57	1452	26.1
Gandul	42.73	4024	94.1
Tras Talleres	68.14	3698	54.2
Condado	197.73	3371	17.1
Campo Alegre	32.36	1827	56.4
Figueroa	86.55	2040	23.5

	Area 1960 (in cuerdas)	Population	Density (per cuerda)
La Zona	105.38	3124	29.6
Condadito	17.46	896	51.3
Pozo del Hato	11.76	376	31.9
Bayola	21.55	444	20.6
Minilla	91.54	2960	32.4
Hipódromo	64.52	3299	51.1
Melilla	33.05	2635	79.7
Marruecos	84.01	11064	131.6
Parque	77.05	2602	33.7
San Mateo	38.15	1912	50.1
Bolívar	46.80	2275	48.6
Buenos Aires	82.09	16947	206.4
San Juan Moderno	21.68	1060	48.8
Pulguero	36.00	2720	75.5
Sagrado Corazón	83.65	2644	31.6
Martin Peña	45.45	904	19.8
Machuchal	35.84	2319	64.7
Chicharo	18.13	1711	94.3
Seboruco	39.39	3949	100.2
Ocean Park	137.46	2780	20.2
Loíza	76.51	3609	47.1
Maria Moczo	27.69	4088	147.6
Monteflores	46.21	1728	37.3
Obrero	232.49	24475	105.2
Villa Palmeras	32.92	4950	150.3
Herrera	31.20	2897	92.8
Las Marias	66.09	870	13.1
Shangai	82.97	18760	226.1
Merhoff	115.81	9538	82.3
Las Palmas	78.85	4711	59.7
Las Casas	169.89	12283	72.2
RIO PIEDRAS			
Gobernador Piñero	2736.61	60959	22.2
Monacillo Urbano	2092.68	18058	8.6
Hato Rey Norte	2155.15	18658	8.6
Hato Rey Sur	512.24	11947	23.3
El Cinco	868.31	6535	7.5
Hato Rey Central	674.65	28745	42.6
Universidad	387.30	4295	11.0
Pueblo	493.50	19591	39.7
Oriente	1124.42	34985	31.1
Sabana Llana Sur	2636.15	10424	3.9
Sabana Llana Norte	1468.00	17906	12.1
San Juan Urban Area	18905.73	432377	22.8

One cuerda = 0.97 acre.
United States Bureau of the Census, 18th Census of Population, 1960.

TABLE 3

Population Change by Ecological Zone, 1950-60

Zone	Population 1950	Population 1960	% Change
Old City	19,655	13,633	−30.6
Beach Front	13,263	14,419	8.5
Central District	74,277	56,719	−20.5
Slum Belt	90,299	85,840	−4.9
Old Suburbs	99,868	144,195	43.3
New Suburbs	32,570	87,908	174.3
San Juan Urban Area	329,932	402,714	22.1

Source: United States Bureau of the Census, 17th and 18th Censuses of Population.

TABLE 4

Population Density by Ecological Zone, 1950 and 1960

Zone	Density 1950 (Per Cuerda)	Density 1960 (Per Cuerda)
Old City	101.8	70.6
Beach Front	21.0	22.8
Central District	52.6	41.8
Slum Belt	96.4	91.6
Old Suburbs	14.3	20.4
New Suburbs	3.9	10.7
San Juan Urban Area	18.4	22.5

Source: United States Bureau of the Census, 17th and 18th Censuses of Population.

TABLE 5

Residential Mobility by Ecological Zone, 1959

Zone	Residential Mobility*
Old City	1.57
Beach Front	1.93
Central District	2.15
Slum Belt	1.63
Old Suburbs	2.10
New Suburbs	1.51

* Number of occupant families March 1, 1955 to March 1, 1959 for dwelling units occupied on March 1, 1955, transcribed from the records of Autoridad de Fuentes Fluviales, based on a two percent sample.

TABLE 6

Mobility by Zone of Destination, 1959

Zone	Type of Mobility*			
	Within Barrio	Inter-Barrio	Inter-Zonal	Other
Old City	47.5	25.0	12.5	15.0
Beach Front	13.3	30.0	35.0	21.7
Central District	10.8	42.9	28.3	17.5
Slum Belt	18.3	43.3	21.7	15.0
Old Suburbs	35.0	31.7	11.7	21.7
New Suburbs	5	10	55	30.0

* A tabulation of last previous addresses for families ordering utility service at a new address during the month of April, 1959. Transcribed from the records of the Autoridad de Fuentes Fluviales, based on a two percent sample.

TABLE 7

Sex Ratio by Ecological Zone, 1960

Zone	Sex Ratio
Old City	118
Beach Front	74
Central District	83
Slum Belt	98
Old Suburbs	89
New Suburbs	96

Source: United States Bureau of the Census, 18th Census of Population.

TABLE 8

Median Age by Ecological Zone, 1950 and 1960

Zone	1950	1960
Old City	24.6	26.8
Beach Front	33.9	31.8
Central District	25.1	24.5
Slum Belt	19.5	17.7
Old Suburbs	24.7	23.9
New Suburbs	20.1	22.6
San Juan Urban Area	23.3	22.7

Source: United States Bureau of the Census, 17th and 18th Censuses of Population.

TABLE 9

Non-White Population by Ecological Zone, 1950*

Zone	Percent of Total
Old City	20
Beach Front	10
Central District	24
Slum Belt	21
Old Suburbs	17
New Suburbs	31
San Juan Urban Area	21

* No enumeration by race or color was made after 1950.
Source: United States Bureau of the Census, 17th Census of Population.

TABLE 10

Income by Ecological Zone, 1950 and 1960

	Per Capita Income, 1950	Median Family Income, 1960
Old City	$607	$2054
Beach Front	963	8439
Central District	614	2544
Slum Belt	395	1597
Old Suburbs	749	3605
New Suburbs	396	4175
San Juan Urban Area	587	3164

Source: United States Bureau of the Census, 17th and 18th Censuses of Population.

TABLE 11

Ratio of Average Income by Ecological Zones to Urban Area Average, 1950 and 1960

	1950	1960
Old City	1.03	0.64
Beach Front	1.64	2.66
Central District	1.04	0.80
Slum Belt	0.67	0.50
Old Suburbs	1.27	1.13
New Suburbs	0.67	1.31

Source: United States Bureau of the Census, 17th and 18th Censuses of Population.

TABLE 12

Rental Values by Ecological Zone, 1960

Zone	Median Contract Monthly Rent
Old City	$ 25
Beach Front	111
Central District	36
Slum Belt	21
Old Suburbs	49
New Suburbs	58

Source: United States Bureau of the Census, 18th Census of Population.

TABLE 13

Type of Occupancy by Ecological Zone, 1960

Zone	Percent of Total Dwelling Units Occupied by Renters
Old City	79.0
Beach Front	46.7
Central District	60.8
Slum Belt	27.4
Old Suburbs	40.8
New Suburbs	16.8

Source: United States Bureau of the Census, 18th Census of Population.

TABLE 14

Automobile Ownership by Ecological Zone, 1960

Zone	Percent of Households with Automobiles
Old City	11.4
Beach Front	73.0
Central District	25.1
Slum Belt	13.1
Old Suburbs	45.7
New Suburbs	59.8

Source: United States Bureau of the Census, 18th Census of Population.

TABLE 15

Recent Construction by Ecological Zone

Zone	Percent Dwelling Units Constructed March 1955 to February 1959*
Old City	4
Beach Front	18
Central District	13
Slum Belt	13
Old Suburbs	49
New Suburbs	56

* Based on ten percent sample taken from meter files of the Puerto Rican Water Resources Authority.

TABLE 16

Housing Units Connected to Public Sewers, 1960

Zone	Percent of all Units Connected
Old City	84.9
Beach Front	66.9
Central District	67.1
Slum Belt	19.2
Old Suburbs	83.4
New Suburbs	68.1

Source: United States Bureau of the Census, 18th Census of Population.

TABLE 17

School Attendance by Ecological Zone, 1950 and 1960

Zone	Percent of Population, Aged 5-24 Enrolled in School	
	1950	1960
Old City	42	54
Beach Front	51	63
Central District	51	59
Slum Belt	37	55
Old Suburbs	52	66
New Suburbs	43	68

Source: United States Bureau of the Census, 17th and 18th Censuses of Population.

TABLE 18

Welfare Aid by Ecological Zone, 1959

Zone	Welfare Cases Per Thousand of the Population*
Old City	38.1
Beach Front	0.7
Central District	32.5
Slum Belt	38.5
Old Suburbs	16.6
New Suburbs	13.8

* Department of Public Welfare, Estado Libre Asociado de Puerto Rico, February 1959.

TABLE 19

Old Age Assistance by Ecological Zone, 1959

Zone	Old Age Assistance Cases Per Thousand of the Population*
Old City	13.9
Beach Front	0.0
Central District	14.7
Slum Belt	13.5
Old Suburbs	6.2
New Suburbs	5.2

* Department of Public Welfare, Estado Libre Asociado de Puerto Rico, February 1959.

TABLE 20

Disability Payments by Ecological Zone, 1959

Zone	Disability Payment Cases Per Thousand of the Population*
Old City	15.4
Beach Front	0.0
Central District	7.6
Slum Belt	9.6
Old Suburbs	3.8
New Suburbs	3.6

* Department of Public Welfare, Estado Libre Asociado de Puerto Rico, February 1959.

TABLE 21

Aid to Dependent Children by Ecological Zone, 1959

Zone	Aided Dependent Children Per Thousand of the Population*
Old City	8.8
Beach Front	0.7
Central District	10.2
Slum Belt	15.4
Old Suburbs	6.5
New Suburbs	5.0

* Department of Public Welfare, Estado Libre Asociado de Puerto Rico, February 1959.

TABLE 22

Juvenile Delinquency by Place of Offense, 1959

Zone	Delinquent Acts Per Thousand of the Population
Old City	0.8
Beach Front	1.0
Central District	0.9
Slum Belt	0.6
Old Suburbs	0.5
New Suburbs	0.3

Source: Office of Statistics, Puerto Rico Police Department.

TABLE 23

Juvenile Delinquency by Residence of the Offender, 1959

Zone	Delinquents Per Thousand of the Population
Old City	1.6
Beach Front	0.4
Central District	1.2
Slum Belt	1.7
Old Suburbs	0.8
New Suburbs	0.5

Source: Office of Statistics, Puerto Rico Police Department.

TABLE 24

Traffic Accidents by Ecological Zone, January, 1959

Zone	Accidents Reported Per 100 Cuerdas
Old City	6.21
Beach Front	6.50
Central District	18.23
Slum Belt	6.51
Old Suburbs	4.08
New Suburbs	0.76

One cuerda = 0.97 acre.
Source: Office of Statistics, Puerto Rico Police Department.

3 Barrios and Neighborhoods

Selection of the Neighborhood Sample

The term neighborhood is commonly used in two senses—
as the smallest recognized subcommunity in a larger community or as a voluntary group centered on an individual
resident. In the latter sense, we may or may not consider the
people around the corner to be neighbors, but we may include those in the next street if the backyards connect. Our
neighbors are people who live across the street, next door,
and a few houses down the block.

Under this definition, the boundaries of the neighborhood
are not precisely ascertainable. Ordinary experience and a
growing body of sociological studies suggest that the intensity of neighboring relationships is greatest for the closest
dwelling units and declines rapidly with increasing distance.

There is no standard number of dwelling units that is appropriate for every cluster of neighboring relationships, but for the purposes of this study, it was decided that each neighborhood would consist of twenty contiguous residences.

A pilot study of the selection process suggested that in the diverse and broken street plan of San Juan, the most convenient method of selecting such a cluster was to start in each case at a street intersection and to move up one street in a predetermined direction, with predetermined rules for dealing with corners, alleys, multiple dwellings and other irregularities.

The area to be sampled was the Urban Area of San Juan, as defined by the United States Bureau of the Census. Area sampling always poses the same dilemmas. A random sample of locations would best be obtained, of course, by overlaying the city map with a system of regular points and then selecting a random sample of these points to be studied. Strict territorial sampling, however, is virtually useless except in territories which have a uniform density of settlement. There are a few such territories—like army camps and public housing projects—but ordinary communities do not conform to this requirement.

Another way of sampling a territory is to list all of the inhabitants and to draw a roster by some random method. This procedure is hampered in most cases by the absence of a list. Attempts to use telephone directories, tax rolls, and other listings which exclude mobile and low income families produce obvious distortions. Ideally, area sampling would be based on small territories of equal population and something like this is achieved in American cities when census enumeration districts are used.

In San Juan, in 1959, the only available sampling districts were the barrios, which are not even approximately uniform in population and area. Nevertheless, no better system was available and we selected our neighborhoods in the following fashion, preserving some element of randomness by a method of selection which left no discretion at all to the selector or the interviewer.

There are fifty-eight barrios. The twenty-nine odd-numbered ones were selected. Through each of these, the longest possible straight line was drawn on the map. The mid-point of that line was plotted. The nearest street intersection to that mid-point was identified on the ground and then the twenty closest dwelling units in a northerly direction from that mid-point were selected for inclusion in the study.[1] Four of these mid-point areas were unacceptable, two on military reservations and two unpopulated. This left a sample of twenty-five neighborhoods of twenty families each—a total of five hundred families. They are described in some detail in the Appendix to this chapter, with a photograph of the site and a chart of the interaction network in each case.

The sample as chosen is a fair representation of the barrios but not of the population, since upper income barrios have smaller populations than lower income barrios. The higher income levels are, therefore, somewhat over-represented.

The Interview Procedure

In each of the twenty households in each of the twenty-five neighborhoods, the housewife was interviewed, usually alone but sometimes in the presence of other family members. This restriction to female respondents again involves some bias. There were three reasons for it. Practically all households in San Juan have adult females—not all have adult males. Housewives are far easier to locate; men are more likely to be absent on work or pleasure. Women have greater direct responsibility for neighboring relationships. They are much more likely than men, for example, to know their children's associates.

Because the neighborhood clusters are small and the research procedure is based upon the reciprocal rating of relationships by both participants, failure to obtain an interview in any case would seriously impair the value of all contiguous cases. We, therefore, attempted a *tour de force*—to reduce the refusal rate to zero. The goal was very nearly achieved. Of the five hundred households originally selected, all five hundred were interviewed. One interview was incomplete because of the mental illness of the respondent, but some information was obtained.

The minimization of refusals may be easier in Puerto Rico, where people are habituated to answering official questionnaires and inquiries, than in other parts of the world. The

[1] Standardized rules for special situations, like multiple dwellings, were designed in advance.

project's procedures included as fanatical an indoctrination of the interviewers as we could contrive, and an elaborate system of callbacks in case of refusal. If the interviewer refused was a man, the callback was made by a woman. If the interviewer refused was a native Puerto Rican, the callback would be made by a Continental. The callback itself was structured as a formal apology. "Señora so-and-so called on you last week and it is obvious she offended you so seriously that you are unwilling to talk to her. I am here to apologize for our Institute and to find out more about this unfortunate incident."

This tactic was not often needed. When used it worked.

The Content of the Interview

The interviews averaged about ninety minutes. Some degree of reticence was encountered in upper class neighborhoods, but generally speaking, respondent cooperation was superlative. Most of the interviewers were college-trained women—young, well-dressed, soft spoken. The usual interview had the character of an unhurried conversation.

The interview schedule (see the Appendix to Chapter 8) was designed to obtain an ample fund of identifying details for all household members: name, age, address, color, family position, earnings, and transportation requirements; for both husband and wife: birthplace, provenance, education, occupation, earnings, other income, length of residence, participation in church and voluntary organizations, identification of close relatives and of work associates, journey to work; for the dwelling unit: number of rooms, room density, housing facilities, residential type, structural type and monthly rent.

The Neighborhood Interaction Scale

The heart of the interview schedule is the Neighborhood Interaction Scale devised by one of the authors in 1948. It was first used in a study of 134 neighborhoods in Minneapolis and St. Paul,[2] and later in a series of studies[3]—1949, 1952 and 1954—of the same block of fifty family dwelling units in a student housing project owned and operated by the University of Minnesota. It has also been used in studies of a California suburb[4] and of urban neighborhoods in Denmark.[5]

There is nothing unusual about this scale. Similar devices have been used by many sociologists to measure neighborhood relationships[6] as well as other forms of voluntary interaction.

[2] Briefly reported in Theodore Caplow and Robert Forman, "Neighborhood Interaction in a Homogeneous Community," *American Sociological Review*, Vol. 15, June 1950, pp. 357-366.
[3] Robert Forman, *A Sociometric Study of Informal Social Participation in a Homogeneous Neighborhood*, unpublished M.A. thesis, University of Minnesota, 1950.

Kenneth L. Shimota, *A Literal Replication of a Sociometric Study of Social Participation in a Homogeneous Neighborhood*, unpublished M.A. thesis, University of Minnesota, 1953.

Thomas D. Cole, *Second Replication of a Sociometric Study of the Interaction of an Informal Group in a Homogeneous Neighborhood*, unpublished M.A. thesis, University of Minnesota, 1955.

These studies by Forman, Shimota, and Cole at three year intervals showed that the pattern of interaction among household units persisted almost unchanged in a rapidly shifting population where turnover was almost complete from each study to the next.
[4] Miriam Brattain, *Neighborhood Relationships in Belle Haven*, unpublished manuscript, 1957.
[5] Kaare Svalastoga, *Nabointeraktion*, Sociometrisk analyse af ni danske naboskab, Copenhagen, 1954.
[6] See among others:

Joel Smith, William H. Form and Gregory P. Stone, "Local Intimacy in a Middle-Sized City," *American Journal of Sociology*, Vol. 60, November 1954, pp. 276-84.

Gregory P. Stone, "City Shoppers and Urban Identification: Observations of the Social Psychology of City Life," *American Journal of Sociology*, Vol. 60, July 1954, pp. 35-45.

Paul Wallin, "A Guttman Scale for Measuring Women's Neighborliness," *American Journal of Sociology*, Vol. 59, November 1953, pp. 241-6.

George A. Lundberg and E. Steele, "Social Attraction Patterns in a Village," *Sociometry*, Vol. 1, 1937, pp. 18-26.

Jessie Bernard, "An Instrument for the Measurement of Neighborhood Relationships with Experimental Applications," *South Western Social Science Quarterly*, September 1937.

Elizabeth Bott, *Family and Social Network, Roles, Norms, and External Relationships in Ordinary Urban Families*, London, Tavistock Publications, 1957, pp. 31-50.

Leon Festinger, Stanley Schachter, and Kurt Back, *Social Pressures in Informal Groups*, New York, Harper and Brothers, 1950.

The Neighborhood Interaction Scale is intended to report existing relationships rather than preferences, in other words, it is a classification of behavior, *not* of attitudes. The subject describes the relationships of his family to every other family within the defined neighborhood, and these are rated by the interviewer on the following scale:

Neighborhood Interaction Scale

Scale Value	Description
0	Do not know their names or faces.
1	Recognize them on the street, but have only a greeting acquaintance.
2	Stop and talk with them outside regularly (involving at least one adult from each family).
3	Stop and talk with them outside regularly (all adults involved).
4	Mutual aid and/or common activities (involving at least one adult from each family).
5	Mutual aid and/or common activities (involving all adults).
6	Mutual visiting and entertaining in each other's houses, including drinking or dining.

This scale can be described as an ordinal scale. Both *a priori* logic and empirical trials indicate that a relationship rated as 2 includes the behavior rated as 1 plus additional behavior, that a relationship rated as 3 includes the behavior rated as 2 plus additional behavior, and so forth. However, we have no basis for assuming that the scale intervals are equal.

We cannot assert that the difference between a rating of 1 and a rating of 2 is meaningfully equivalent to the difference between a rating of 2 and a rating of 3. On the other hand, they are *numerically* equivalent—because we made them so —and with certain precautions, we can treat the ratings produced by this scale *as if* it were an interval scale. In other words, we shall usurp the privilege of adding, subtracting, multiplying and dividing scores based on these numbers. Most of our results will therefore have a built-in error. We suppose that this error will be too small to distort the findings, and we can make a pretty good case for this supposition in general, without being able to prove it in any particular instance.

Ambience Measurements

Ambience is a term sometimes used for an unorganized group related by a network of interaction. Strictly speaking, an ambience is the collectivity of all persons interacting with a designated subject in a designated context.[6] Thus, all the neighbors with whom a given subject sustains interaction above a stated minimum level comprise a meaningful collectivity, whose members are not necessarily in interaction with each other. In some cases the members of these collectivities are completely disconnected and have no mutual relationships except through the subject. In other instances, each member may sustain interaction with many others.

Each of our interviews describes the neighborhood ambience of a given household. What we call *the neighborhood* —the entire network of inter-relations among the twenty households—is actually a cluster of mutually dependent ambiences. Useem and Gibson call this the *immediate neighborhood* and describe it thus:

Neighbors, as designated by the men of our sample, are the adult occupants of households in close proximity to themselves. Each man conceived of himself and his wife as the center of his neighbors; and thus those immediately surrounding him are denoted as "my" neighbors, "our" neighbors, or the people living "next to us." Such persons are usually spatially and visibly accessible to the man and his wife. This would imply that, unless there is ecological separation of a small number of home units from other units, each contiguous household in a densely settled area will have an overlapping but slightly different set of neighbors.[7]

Ambiences are interesting to work with. They can be treated geometrically or graphically or algebraically. Their analyses sometimes generate extraordinary mathematical complications.[8] It can be shown, for example, that in a neighbor-

[6] Theodore Caplow, "Definition and Measurement of the Ambience," *Social Forces*, Vol. 34, October 1955.
[7] Ruth Hill Useem, John Useem, and Duane L. Gibson, "The Function of Neighboring for the Middle-Class Male," *Human Organization*, Vol. 19, Summer, 1960, p. 69.
[8] One especially useful model is provided by Graph Theory. Frank Harary and Robert G. Norman, *Graph Theory as a Mathematical Model in Social Science*. Ann Arbor, Michigan, Institute for Social Research, 1953.

hood of 20 units the number of possible pair relationships (between units, not persons) is $\dfrac{n\,(n-1)}{2}$ or 190.

However, this is merely the beginning. There are also the relationships to be measured between individuals and sub-groups of various sizes, and among these sub-groups. If all of these are combined, then the number of *potential* relationships in a population of N at a given time equals $\dfrac{3^n - 2^n + 1}{2}$.

Our little group of twenty families has the staggering total of 1,742,867,913 potential relationships.

Clearly, any interactional network is inherently complicated, although we may simplify it for analysis. The principal measures that are used in this study are:

1. *Extensity of Neighboring*—The number of families with whom a subject family interacts.
2. *Interaction Outscore*—The sum of the ratings of the relationships *reported by a subject family* with its neighbors.[9]
3. *Interaction Inscore*—The sum of the ratings of all relationships with a subject family *reported by its neighbors*.
4. *Confirmed Interaction Score*—The sum of ratings of all relationships reported by a subject family with its neighbors and confirmed by their reports.

A measure of neighboring *Intensity* is obtained by dividing each family's Confirmed Interaction Score by the number of neighbors with whom it has confirmed relationships.

This use of confirmed scores requires a word of explanation. Neighbors do not always agree on the intimacy of their relationships. Some discrepancies are due to faults of memory and some are attributable to interviewer error, but there is also reason to think that discrepancies may be socially meaningful.[10]

Because both members of every related pair in this sample were interviewed, we can compute a minimum intimacy

[9] For example, if there are fourteen neighbors whom they do not know at all, two neighbors with whom they have only a greeting acquaintance and three neighbors with whom they exchange visits and entertainment, the family's total outscore is 20.
[10] The theory of the matter is admirably set forth in Peter M. Blau, "Patterns of Choice in Interpersonal Relations" *American Sociological Review*, Vol. 27, February 1962.

on which both participants agree. For example, if neighbor A describes a relationship at a level of 6 with neighbor B (mutual visiting and entertaining) and neighbor B describes a less intimate relationship, at the level of 4 (common activities involving one adult from each family), we may say that they agree about the existence of a relationship with an intimacy of *at least* 4 and this figure enters the Confirmed Interaction Score of each family.

Of course, this measure is only a rough approximation to the measurement of interaction by an objective observer. We will have more to say in a later chapter about the possible interpretation of discrepancies.

The Nature of the Neighboring Relationship

Good neighbors, say the Useems and Gibson[11] are friendly but not friends. The norms of their situation includes obligations of emergency aid, mutual assistance, borrowing and lending, respect for privacy, and the maintenance of collective appearances.

It appears that to our subjects—like the people represented in the North American studies—neighboring constitutes a definite and separable field of relationships. The interaction networks we have traced are composed of these relationships and these only. Kinship, occupational, affectional and other ties can exist between persons who are neighbors also, but these have not been taken into account in this report. When we speak here of an intimate relationship between two families we mean intimacy based on residential propinquity and in the role of neighbors. What makes this procedure possible is that our subjects recognize the same distinction and make it themselves.

[11] *Op. cit.*

Structural Diversities

The Appendix to this chapter contains a description and photograph of each neighborhood and an interaction chart based on the Neighborhood Interaction Scale. These charts are circular sociograms, one for each of the neighborhoods studied. Each chart has twenty squares arranged in a circle. Each square represents one household. Spatial relationships have been generally but not perfectly represented.

The lines on the chart connect pairs of dwelling units. These lines stand for active confirmed relationships between a pair of families. An active relationship has a scale value of 2 or more. Trivial relationships (having a scale value of 1) have been omitted for the sake of readability. Relationships with scale values of 4 or more (close or intimate relationships) are represented by solid lines, other active relationships by dotted lines.

At the bottom of each chart are shown the number of active confirmed relationships in the neighborhood, and the proportion of these that are close relationships. The number of relationships ranges from a low of 5 in La Zona, where most families are completely isolated, to 190 in Marina, where the theoretical maximum is achieved.

Looking at these networks, one gets the sensation of peering through a microscope at some new species of organism. The networks differ greatly in structure, and the differences matter. However, it is not easy to interpret what we see as we examine them. Except for a small number of sociometric terms which are partly applicable to this kind of social fabric, there is no standard classification for interaction networks and no quick way of seizing the implications of the fact that some urban dwellers are involved in vast clusters of local relationships, while others are as isolated as they might be on a desert island.

Several major patterns appear in this sample:

1. The Tribal pattern is represented by Marina, Pueblo, and Puerta de Tierra. There are few isolates in these neighborhoods, everyone knows everyone else and associates actively with nearly everyone else. The neighborhood is an extension of the family. It exerts continuous

social influence and absorbs a large part of the free time
and energy of its residents. There are no exclusive
cliques. Monacillo Urbano represents a variant in which
the tribal pattern is incomplete, with six families who
have no close relationships.

2. The Intimate pattern, as found in Bolivar, and Parque,
   is marked by the predominance of intimate over non-
   intimate relationships. In the remarkable case of Bolivar,
   although the average relationship has a scale value of
   more than four, there are not many casual contacts.
   Nearly every family is involved in a few close relationships. Most of these are with immediately adjacent
   neighbors, but they overlap sufficiently to form a network.

3. The Casual pattern, as in Seboruco and Minilla, shows
   a fairly complete, fairly symmetrical cluster of predominantly casual relationships. There are few isolates and
   few stars. Most families participate in several relationships, and overlapping brings each household into social
   proximity with every other even when they are not directly related.

4. The Clique pattern appears in Monteflores, Loíza, and
   Mercado. Many families are completely isolated. The
   neighborhood network is centered on a small clique of
   closely interrelated households to which the remaining
   households in the neighborhood are loosely connected,
   without being extensively related to each other. Relationships within the clique are mostly intimate while
   relationships between clique members and non-mem-
   bers are mostly casual. Isolation may be a function of
   physical distance from a clique center, or of deviant
   social characteristics. Sagrado Corazón, Hato Rey Sur,
   and Merhoff all display multiple cliques. In the case of
   Sagrado Corazón there are two separate, fairly dense
   networks of casual relationships having a single family
   in common. The interaction pattern for Merhoff de-
   vides in half and one of the halves shows two tight
   cliques which do not overlap.

5. The Ring-Around-the-Rosie pattern is illustrated by
   Las Casas where almost every family has an intimate
   relationship with one or two close neighbors. Neighboring is based on immediate contiguity, so that most of
   the households are unconnected with most of the others.

6. The Anomie pattern is represented in this sample by
   the spectacular case of La Zona with twelve isolated

and thirteen partially isolated families. This type of neighborhood is not a meaningful social entity.

The origins of these diverse patterns are unclear. There does not seem to be any simple explanation of why they differ so much. The variation in the intensity of neighborhood interaction observed among our twenty-five neighborhoods has been checked against every known characteristic of their resident populations without uncovering any significant correlations. This is perhaps to be expected, since the sample of neighborhoods (as distinct from the sample of families) is very small. Even if we did have more information about our twenty-five neighborhoods of twenty families each, it is unlikely that their structural diversity could be understood without reference to the larger neighborhoods of 50, 100, or 500 families to which they belong.

The twenty-five sociograms show some extraordinary contrasts. Consider, for example, the difference between the interwoven web of cross-relationships in Neighborhood II (known to the interviewers as The Rabbit Warren) and the complete absence of intimate relationships in Neighborhood VI.

It is tempting to suppose that such gross differences can only be explained in terms of gross social characteristics. We might guess, for example, that Neighborhood II illustrates the swarming gregariousness of the poor, and Neighborhood VI the aloof exclusiveness of the rich, or that Neighborhood II is an old neighborhood of solidly-rooted and inter-married families, while Neighborhood VI is composed of recent settlers. Such simple explanations would be helpful if they worked, but examination of the data reveals they do not. Each beautiful theory is assailed by a gang of brutal facts. The puzzle of differential neighborhood structure is not so easily solved until we examine the characteristics of individual families, taken separately, and it is this task to which we turn in the following chapter.

APPENDIX

*Photographs, Descriptions, and Interaction
Networks—The Twenty-Five Neighborhoods*

Neighborhood 1—BARRIO MERCADO

The first neighborhood studied is located in Mercado, one of the oldest sections of Old San Juan. Originally, the area was composed of middle-class residences with adjoining servant's quarters. In characteristic Spanish colonial style, the buildings extended to the edge of a narrow sidewalk, enclosing an interior patio well shaded from the tropical sun. Later, extensive sub-division of these old units brought the population density to an incredible figure for one-story buildings (210 persons per acre in 1960).

Although Mercado is overcrowded and noisy, and contains the accumulated dirt of more than four centuries, it is a preferred location for its lower-class inhabitants, most of whom have experienced a relatively high degree of social mobility. More wives than husbands, but a majority of both, are of rural origin. When the men were about twenty-five and the women twenty and the latter usually married for the first time, they migrated to San Juan. They first settled in the Slum Belt of Santurce, then moved to a "better slum" in Old San Juan, and rose into the most exclusive of all slums, La Perla, and thence, to their present location.

La Perla is situated on the side of a hill very convenient to and yet isolated from the business district. With the city behind it, a vast expanse of ocean in front, a refreshing sea-breeze, and plenty of bright sunlight, it is no wonder that "The Pearl" has an informal waiting list of would-be tenants. Almost by design La Perla represents the last step before the upwardly mobile enter the world of lower-class respectability. When the tenants of Mercado talk about La Perla, it is with the wistfulness of exiles, who have lived in another world, left it and cannot return.

Mobility into Mercado does have some compensations however. Stone structures are generally preferable to those made of wood. The address is now justifiably San Juan. The larger community now recognizes one's existence and income rises.

The men of Mercado are employed in minor clerical positions and skilled trades. Twenty-five percent of the households have no male head, and many of the women practice prostitution.

Mercado is not an integrated social unit. There are no intimate cliques and only an average number of intimate social relationships. Three of the families have no close relationships with any of their neighbors.

How do these people feel about Mercado after having left the country, moved up the urban ladder and escaped from the slum environment? Half of them describe Mercado as a "good place to live." The other half still have mobility in mind, and plan to move to some part of Central Santurce or even to a suburb.

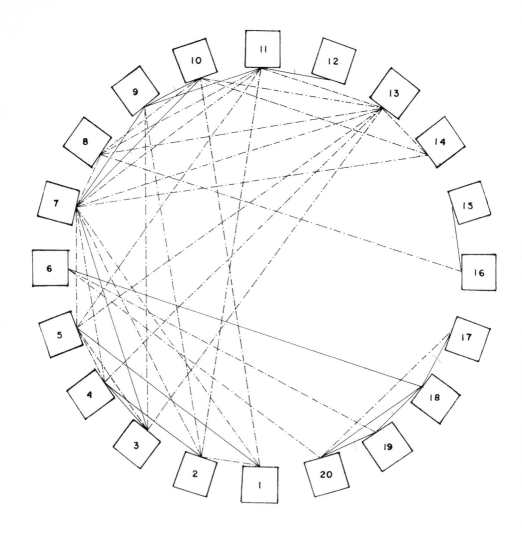

Neighborhood 1—BARRIO MERCADO

		Number
—·—·	Confirmed (casual) relationships scored 2-3	30
———	Confirmed (intimate) relationships scored 4-5-6	15
	Total	45

Neighborhood 2—BARRIO LA MARINA

Unlike the Mercado residents who have made the leap out of the slum, the families of Marina, the other neighborhood studied in Old San Juan, are those who have remained behind. Most of the men were born in rural areas, but the women have had a different history. A majority of them were born in the Metropolitan Area and half of these in Old San Juan itself. They have not experienced much upward mobility.

Marina is an area of converted warehouses close to the harbor. Access to the business district is more difficut than from Mercado. Most of the structures were built prior to World War I and most of them are still used as warehouses. During the day, the streets are filled with residents and warehouse workers. At night, the district becomes a refuge for vagrants and alcoholics, whom the residents avoid by arriving home before dark, and staying inside.

The interior of the building where our twenty families live is like a maze. Apartments are not clearly defined. The families live more or less intertwined, in apparent harmony. Examples of mutual aid and support were frequently witnessed. This is the most integrated neighborhood we studied. Regardless of the index used—volume, intensity or number of relationships—Marina ranks above all others.

For the majority of the inhabitants, this social environment is enjoyable and no thought of moving arises. A small minority feel themselves caught in a trap—or a maze. While they ostensibly behave as the others, they whispered complaints to the interviewer. The expression of dissatisfaction is too great a threat to the neighborhood to be allowed.

Like a middle-class suburb, Marina requires a high degree of behavioral conformity, though with perhaps more justification. Most families have children; most household heads work in Old San Juan; most follow domestic and service occupations; most go to church regularly; most children don't go to school regularly; most of the neighbors are good; most have the same customs; and most are going to be here for a long time.

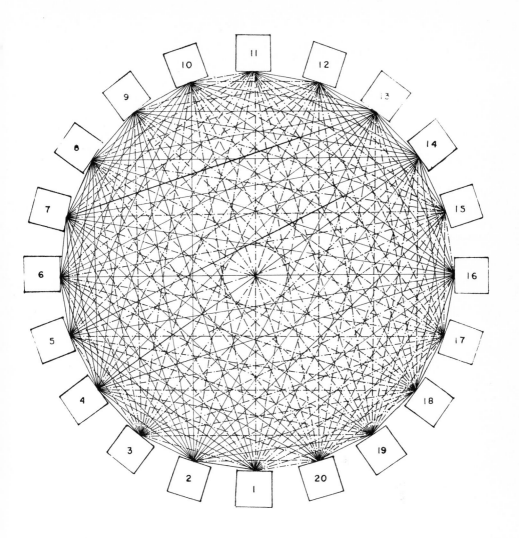

Neighborhood 2—BARRIO MARINA

		Number
— . — ·	Confirmed (casual) relationships scored 2-3	108
——	Confirmed (intimate) relationships scored 4-5-6	81
	Total	189

Neighborhood 3—BARRIO PUERTA DE TIERRA

Puerta de Tierra is located just outside Old San Juan near the harbor naval installation. Built in 1948-50, this public project appears monotonous, overcrowded and dreary. The courtyards are barren and children prefer to play in the street.

The average household consists of five persons. Thirty percent have no male head, and there are many children. The average educational attainment is five years. Reported income is the lowest of any neighborhood in the study. This must be interpreted with caution, however. Many families conceal their real incomes to prevent a raise in their rent.

Ten percent are non-white. Almost all of the men were born in rural Puerto Rico. The typical household head came to San Juan more than twenty years ago, lived in at least two slums and then moved to the housing project. In practically every case, the last previous address was in the same barrio.

The migration pattern for women is somewhat different. More of them were born in the metropolitan area, and those born in the country have fewer years of urban residence than their men.

Most household heads work in San Juan, walking to their places of work. They are employed in semi-skilled and unskilled occupations. Schools, shops, public transportation, churches and other facilities are convenient. This is one reason why sixty-five percent consider their project a good place to live and most of the remainder are moderately satisfied, too. Sixty-five percent of the families plan to stay permanently.

The social network of Puerta de Tierra is quite loose. There are many more casual than close relationships.

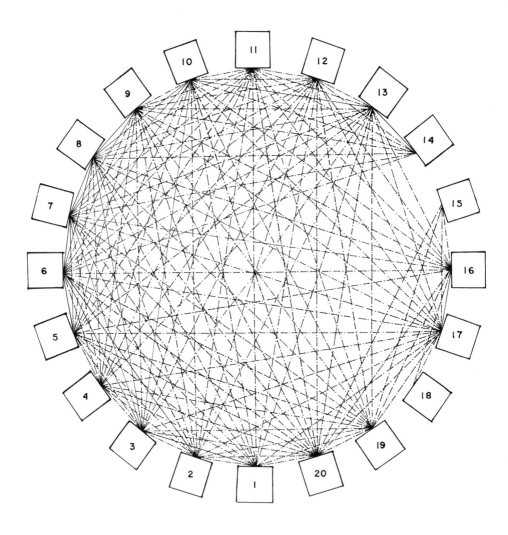

Neighborhood 3 — BARRIO PUERTA DE TIERRA

		Number
— · — · Confirmed (casual) relationships scored 2-3		127
——— Confirmed (intimate) relationships scored 4-5-6		19
	Total	146

Neighborhood 4—BARRIO MIRAMAR

Although Miramar does not face the ocean, it borders Laguna Condado and belongs in the ecological zone of the Beachfront. It differs from Parque and Las Marias (the other two Beachfront neighborhoods in the sample) in being older and less exclusively residential.

Upper and middle-class in composition, Miramar is located at the western edge of Santurce between the two principal downtown avenues —Ponce de Leon and Fernandez Juncos. The population is an interesting mixture of old Puerto Rican families who occupy single family houses built around 1920 and semi-transients who occupy the high rise apartment buildings and guest houses. As land values rise and facilities for short term visitors further encroach on this neighborhood, more displacement to the suburbs takes place. To some extent this movement is reduced by a fierce sentiment among old Miramar residents that anyone who sells out is a traitor to his neighbors.

The residents of Miramar have an average educational attainment of one year of college. Most family heads are professionals who work in Old San Juan and their income is high. Twenty-five percent of the men were born in the urban area and forty percent outside Puerto Rico. The women show similar origins, with a slightly larger proportion from rural Puerto Rico.

Only one-fifth of the families report a previous address in rural Puerto Rico. The typical family moved to Miramar some ten years ago from another part of Santurce. There are relatively few children in these families, and few working wives. Relatives outside the nuclear family often live in the same household. The dominant type in Miramar is a middle-aged, middle-class professional couple, whose children are grown.

With the mixture of single and multiple dwellings, old and new residents, Puerto Ricans and Continentals, the volume and intensity of neighboring are quite low. There are no cliques and many families are isolated. Ninety percent of the residents consider their neighborhood a good place to live and only twenty percent expect ever to move.

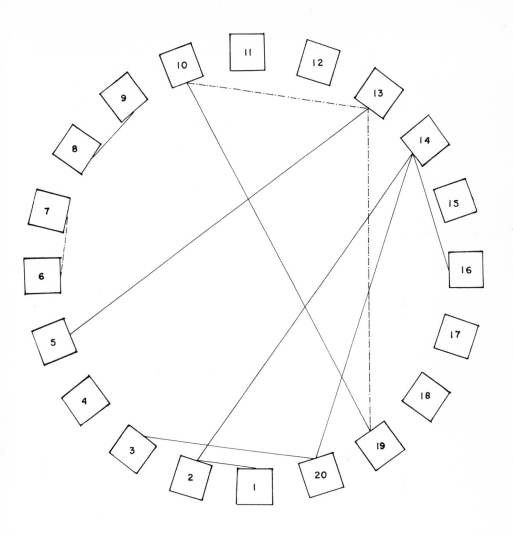

Neighborhood 4—BARRIO MIRAMAR

		Number
—·—·	Confirmed (casual) relationships scored 2-3	3
——	Confirmed (intimate) relationships scored 4-5-6	8
	Total	11

*Neighborhood 5—*BARRIO CAMPO ALEGRE

Elsewhere we have observed the ribbon development of the central business district in Santurce. One result of this phenomenon may have been to protect residential neighborhoods from change. Since there has been invasion but little succession, many parts of the city represent a blend of former epochs. Campo Alegre is an example.

This neighborhood is located only one block from the central business district, on an old and narrow road. The structures vary in age from five to fifty years. They vary in type from upper-class apartments to dilapidated hovels.

There are two distinct patterns of migration—related to whether a family has children. The typical family with children arrived in San Juan about eleven years ago. They lived in two other neighborhoods in Santurce and moved to Campo Alegre from an adjacent barrio. The typical family without children has experienced more mobility. They lived in at least three other areas of Old San Juan or Santurce before moving to their present address about fifteen years ago.

The volume of neighboring is slightly above average. Nine families have no close relationship with their neighbors, and there is one partial clique. Most of the residents are mildly satisfied. They say: "it is located near my work," "churches are close, everything is at hand, if you don't have a car, you don't suffer." But a few less enthusiastic residents complained about their neighbors: "the people here have a bad reputation, it is a bad neighborhood, the dogs bark a lot."

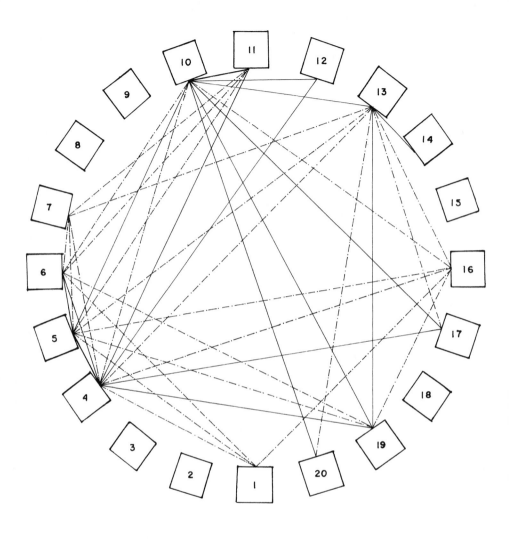

Neighborhood 5 — BARRIO CAMPO ALEGRE

		Number
— · — ·	Confirmed (casual) relationships scored 2-3	24
——	Confirmed (intimate) relationships scored 4-5-6	16
	Total	40

Neighborhood 6—BARRIO LA ZONA

La Zona borders the canal on the south, the Bayamon Highway on the west and a heavy commercial trafficway (Avenida Fernandez Juncos) to the north. To the east, it merges with the rest of the slum belt. Transportation is easily accessible but the elevation is low, and the area is physically undesirable.

The streets are not paved, but are wider than other slums. There are no sidewalks, street lighting is poor, and the smell from the Canal pervades the district. The unpainted wooden houses are built on pilings and have swampy puddles under them.

The area ranks high in crime and delinquency. Syphilitics, prostitutes, drunkards and stray dogs are common sights. Men without shirts parade the streets, or work on their cars while drinking beer, or nap on the "sidewalk" undisturbed by the flies and insects. "Hi-fi's" from some of the houses blast in competition with the juke-boxes from the coffee shops and pool halls.

The population density is nearly seventy persons per acre. Most structures are single family dwellings which may be occupied by as many as six families. The average household consists of five persons. There are more than three persons per bedrocm. Educational attainment is low— an average of five years. Per capita income is about six dollars per week. Most of the men are semi-skilled workers employed in Santurce.

After their household duties are completed in some fashion, women appear at ease on the streets, or remain at a balcony or window. They often leave La Zona during the day to go to the *centro*, or visit the cinema. Church attendance is low.

This area was settled much earlier than Merhoff (our other slum neighborhood), and the respondents here are older. Most of them were born outside the Metropolitan Area but have lived in San Juan for twenty or more years. They moved to their present address from another in or near the same barrio seven years ago, on the average.

La Zona stands at the bottom of our sample in neighborhood satisfaction and social integration. The neighbors are not friendly towards each other. There are few intimate or even casual relationships. Only a third of the families plan to remain in their present homes. These findings are not difficult to understand.

First, the physical conditions in La Zona are the worst observed. Respondents complain continually about their neighborhood. "The toilet stinks terribly. The rent is very high for the discomfort . . . in which we live." "The house is a miserable room—dirty, uncomfortable, lots of bugs."

These people have been frustrated in their attempts at mobility. Twenty years of urban residence finds them in La Zona, perhaps as badly off as they were in the country, with hope for improvement fading. There is not much left to expect but more filth, insults, fights, and misery. By now they have given up trying.

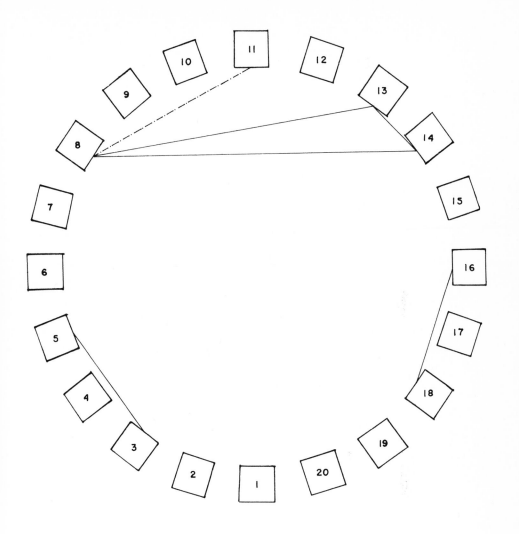

Neighborhood 6 — BARRIO LA ZONA

		Number
—.—.	Confirmed (casual) relationships scored 2-3	1
——	Confirmed (intimate) relationships scored 4-5-6	4
	Total	5

*Neighborhood 7—*BARRIO POZO DEL HATO

As previously noted, the sample contains great variety, including a neighborhood that no longer exists. When we interviewed the residents of Pozo del Hato, clearance had recently begun for the extension of Avenida Baldorioty de Castro. Since that time, the construction has been completed and the new expressway now runs through the neighborhood.

The impending removal undoubtedly affected the responses of our subjects. They had resigned themselves to moving and the neighborhood was already filled with the noise and dirt of heavy construction equipment. Nevertheless, we thought it worthwhile to study this neighborhood as an example of the relocation process under way throughout the city.

The buildings in Pozo del Hato were constructed shortly before World War II. Most of them were lower class multiple dwellings. The neighborhood was located about halfway between Avenida Ashford and Ponce de Leon Avenue at the western edge of Santurce.

Nearly half of the families were non-white. Educational attainment was average and income low. There were 4.6 persons per family and thirty percent lacked a male head. Nearly all the adults were born in rural Puerto Rico. The typical resident came to San Juan about fifteen years ago, and to Pozo del Hato five years ago.

The principal place of employment was located about half a mile away, and two-thirds of the people walked to work. Almost all urban amenities were distant enough for an inconveniently long walk but not far enough away to require transportation. This partial inaccessibility seemed to account for an unenthusiastic evaluation of the neighborhood. Three out of ten respondents said it was not a good place to live.

The disorganizing influence of the demolition program is seen in the interaction network. Half of the families were socially isolated, there were no cliques and the extensity of neighboring was very low. From the comments made by the respondents, the interaction pattern of the neighborhood was quite different before relocation began.

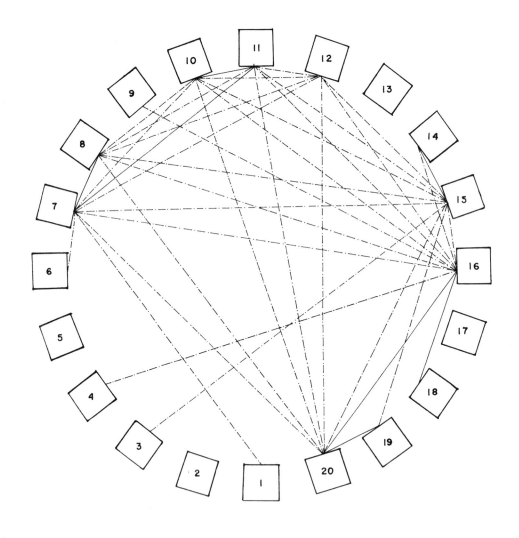

Neighborhood 7 — POZO DEL HATO

		Number
— · — ·	Confirmed (casual) relationships scored 2-3	31
——	Confirmed (intimate) relationships scored 4-5-6	7
	Total	38

Neighborhood 8—BARRIO MINILLA

This neighborhood is a forgotten area in the center of the city. The government drafted plans to construct a government office on the site, purchased this land and demolished many houses some years ago. For one reason or another the program was abandoned after some of the clearance had been completed and the area now waits for the government to make further decisions. The present residents of the district live in the few remaining houses, surrounded by a large belt of vacant land.

From the doorsteps of any of these houses one sees first the vestiges of the destroyed buildings, then a series of parking lots for downtown office workers, and finally, the tall buildings of the new business center. In this state of frozen transition, the residents lead a quite comfortable life. They are middle and lower class families whose household size, education, occupation, and income are just below the average of all families in our sample.

About two-thirds of both husbands and wives were born in rural Puerto Rico. The typical family moved to their present address nine years ago, from a nearby section of Santurce. The average intensity of neighboring is quite low. There are few close relationships and several of the families are isolated.

They apparently do not object to this pattern of neighboring. Most of them are satisfied with the neighborhood. "It is not the most enchanting street but it is centrally located, close to the bus, churches, movies, drugstores, and clothing stores, etc. It is also very quiet." "You can see the city and the people here mind their own business but help you when necessary." "There have never been any problems."

Most of the residents plan to remain in their homes unless the government decides to continue with its clearance program. Only fifteen percent had definite plans to move at the time of the interview.

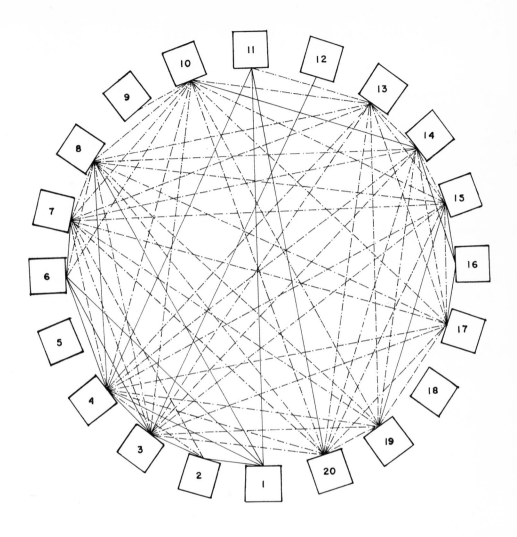

*Neighborhood 8—*BARRIO MINILLAS

		Number
—.—.	Confirmed (casual) relationships scored 2-3	57
——	Confirmed (intimate) relationships scored 4-5-6	19
	Total	76

Neighborhood 9—BARRIO MELILLA

A neighborhood can be too close to the amenities of the city. Located near Stop 22, near the center of the business district, Melilla contains a variety of functions; bars, hospitals, stores, and warehouses. In former years, the neighborhood was well separated from the business district. The respondents, many of whom have lived in the neighborhood for twenty years or more, wistfully recall these earlier conditions.

The population is mixed middle and lower class in composition. The average household consists of four persons, including many children. Educational attainment and per capita income are moderately high, reflecting long urban tenure. Most of the men are employed in minor professional and managerial positions in eastern Santurce or Old San Juan. The typical family moved to its present address from an adjacent barrio nearly twelve years ago.

With the difficult physical conditions in the neighborhood, social relationships are very poorly developed. Thirteen families are isolated, and there is a single clique.

The following comments by residents of Melillia are typical in tone: "Yes, the neighborhood is a good place to live, there are good neighbors but the house of prostitution on the corner has ruined the place." "The location is very convenient, but the area is deteriorating because of so many shops and a lot of traffic." "I hate it, the neighbors across the street are noisy, there are too many bars and drunkards around here."

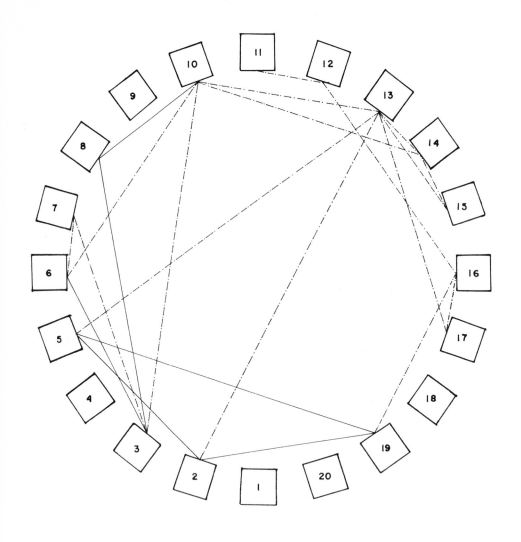

Neighborhood 9 — BARRIO MELILLA

		Number
— · — ·	Confirmed (casual) relationships scored 2-3	16
——	Confirmed (intimate) relationships scored 4-5-6	6
	Total	22

Barrio Parque consists of one and two-story homes, built between World War I and World War II. Most of the houses represent a compromise between Latin and North American plans. Each house has at least a small front yard, but the rear is enclosed by walls to make a patio.

The average household has four persons. Both husband and wife report slightly more than one year of college. Most of the men are employed in professional and sales work, while their wives remain at home. The majority drive their own cars to an office in Santurce.

There are two distinct patterns regarding migration. Half of the wives and one-third of the husbands were born in rural Puerto Rico. They migrated to San Juan shortly before World War II and moved to their present addresses about ten years ago. In the other pattern, both husbands and wives were born outside Puerto Rico, most of them in the United States. They lived at another address in San Juan for a short period, and then moved to Parque six or seven years ago.

The proximity of the beach, the absence of through traffic, and the social homogeneity of the residents seem to produce fairly intense neighboring. Among the twenty-four neighborhoods studied, Parque ranks fifth in this regard. Almost every family reports two or three close relationships with neighbors and these overlap to form a fairly well integrated social network.

Neighborhood satisfaction is quite high. Only one resident expressed dissatisfaction. She said: "There are a lot of thieves who have broken into our house four or five times. The condition of the street is terrible. The city has been repaving it for months and hasn't finished yet. This is a very noisy location and there are a lot of mosquitoes." It is noteworthy that her negative remarks included nothing against her neighbors. The overwhelming majority consider the neighbors "highly educated," "agreeable," "cordial," "decent," "reserved," and "ones who mind their own business." The neighborhood is described as "centrally located," "quiet," "close to the beach," and "healthy."

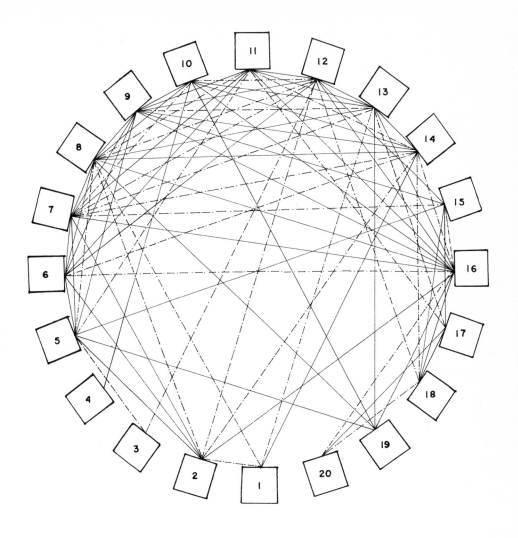

Neighborhood 10—BARRIO PARQUE

		Number
—·—·	Confirmed (casual) relationships scored 2-3	30
——	Confirmed (intimate) relationships scored 4-5-6	51
	Total	81

Bolivar is a neighborhood of older owner-occupied single family houses, located near one end of the central business district. There are scattered upper and lower class residents, but the great majority are middle class. What Bolivar lacks in social heterogeneity, however, it makes up in its mixture of land uses. A small plaza, a private school, a movie theater, a small grocery store, and a small factory are found in the immediate vicinity of the neighborhood.

Sixty-five percent of the current residents moved to Bolivar from a previous address in Santurce. The women have been somewhat more mobile than the men. Sixty percent of them were born in the rural sections, and twenty-five percent outside Puerto Rico, several in another Spanish-speaking Caribbean island.

The primary disadvantage of the neighborhood is that it is too close to everything, including one of the main avenues of transportation, Fernandez Juncos. The noise of traffic, school children, moviegoers, grocery shoppers, factory workers, and plaza loafers is deafening throughout the day and most of the night. Neighborhood satisfaction is understandably low. Forty-five percent of the families definitely plan to move, and another fifteen percent plan to do so when resources are available. The remaining forty percent express only qualified satisfaction: "The neighbors couldn't be better but this house faces the plaza and at night there is a lot of noise, fights, and so forth."

Low neighborhood satisfaction and mixed land use have not inhibited neighboring at all. Many residents of Bolivar have five or six intimate relationships with their neighbors. There are no cliques, and only two families are isolated.

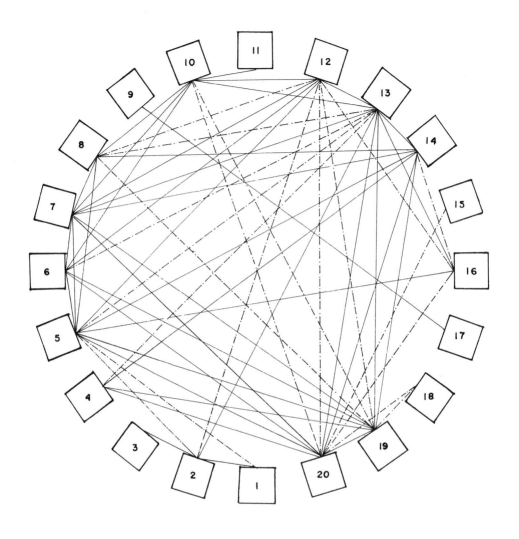

Neighborhood 11 — BARRIO BOLIVAR

		Number
—·—·	Confirmed (casual) relationships scored 2-3	19
——	Confirmed (intimate) relationships scored 4-5-6	40
	Total	59

Neighborhood 12—BARRIO SAN JUAN MODERNO

In order to see the real beauty of San Juan—its plazas, hidden patios, isolated gardens—one must abandon the car and walk slowly through the streets. Nowhere is this more clearly demonstrated than in the neighborhood of San Juan Moderno. Although it is located only a block away from a major traffic thoroughfare, it is not easily accessible to the stranger.

Most of the structures in the neighborhood are multi-family dwellings built between World War I and World War II. They are located on a dead end street in a residential area of middle and lower class composition. The average household size is the smallest of any neighborhood in our study, only three persons. There are very few children, but a number of households include adult relatives. Forty percent of the households have no male head.

The average educational attainment is quite high, 11.6 years. Half of the husbands and wives were born outside metropolitan San Juan and migrated to the city fifteen or twenty years ago, and to San Juan Moderno about five years ago.

The neighborhood is a closely knit unit. On a casual level, nearly everyone here knows some of his neighbors. When we examine closer relationships we find two separate cliques—both of which are nearly closed groups. Only three families are uncommitted to one clique or the other.

When asked if she considers this neighborhood a good place to live every respondent was enthusiastic. The neighborhood was typically described by comments like these: "The neighbors are really a family." "Only decent people live here." "People mind their own business except when one needs help, then we all help each other." "Everything is nearby—clothing stores, drugstores, stores of all kinds."

It is not surprising to learn that ninety percent of the families plan to remain in their present homes.

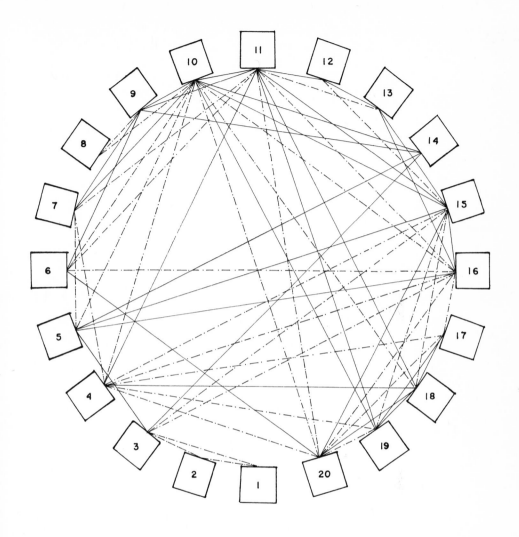

Neighborhood 12 — BARRIO SAN JUAN MODERNO

		Number
— · — · Confirmed (casual) relationships scored 2-3		33
——— Confirmed (intimate) relationships scored 4-5-6		31
	Total	64

Neighborhood 13—BARRIO SAGRADO CORAZÓN DE JESUS

In this barrio—Sagrado Corazón de Jesus (The Sacred Heart of Jesus)—the families studied have remained for an average of thirty years. Aside from the name, what is so attractive about this neighborhood that keeps its residents from leaving?

Almost all the amenities of urban living are present. The streets and sidewalks are well paved, clean and lighted, free from heavy traffic. There is little noise and no bad odors. Public transportation is available two blocks away and there is ample parking space for automobiles. Schools, grocery stores, pharmacies, variety stores, and parks are all within walking distance. Hucksters selling fruit, vegetables, eggs, milk and other provisions pass daily. The neighborhood is situated on a hill where the breeze blows constantly.

The one and two story buildings are occupied predominantly by lower middle class families. There are no non-residential land uses in the immediate area. Thirty percent of the households have no male head, and there are few children. The women are older than average.

Educational attainment is surprisingly high, given the age and occupations of the residents. Some of these women may have reduced their level of living after a husband's death. About half of the men and three-fourths of the women were born in rural Puerto Rico. Most of them lived in several places in the Metropolitan Area before moving to Sagrado Corazón.

Once again we find a case where social integration is fairly low and neighborhood satisfaction high. There are two separate, fairly dense networks of casual relationships, having only one family in common. When we consider only intimate relationships, these networks disappear, leaving five exclusive pair relationships, and ten isolated families.

The residents of Sagrado Corazón are unqualifiedly enthusiastic about their neighborhood.

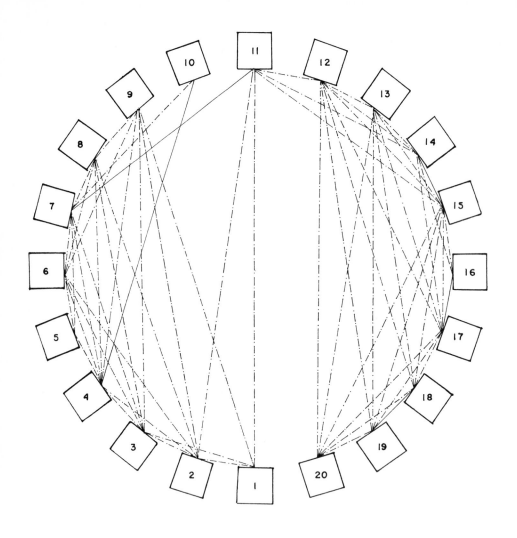

Neighborhood 13—BARRIO SAGRADO CORAZON

		Number
—·—·	Confirmed (casual) relationships scored 2-3	56
——	Confirmed (intimate) relationships scored 4-5-6	5
	Total	61

Neighborhood 14—BARRIO MACHUCHAL

It is easy to drive past this neighborhood and not see it. The houses are sandwiched between gas stations, bars, and auto repair shops, on a street just off a major expressway. There is no sign that anyone cares for this area, inhabitants or planners. Machuchal seems to be a haphazard conglomeration of unrelated uses.

Neighboring is low. Nine of the families have no close relationship with any neighbor.

Yet Machuchalites would have it no other way. The typical family moved here eight years ago from another Santurce neighborhood and has little intention of leaving. Their satisfaction is explained by the peculiar advantages which this location offers their particular needs.

Families in Machuchal either lack children, or wives, or husbands. In the rare case where a husband and wife live together without children, one or both of the spouses are engaged in some illegal occupation. Women living with their children here are likely to be prostitutes. The men here are likely to be living with mistresses.

Precisely because the larger community does not approve of their occupations or their living arrangements, the residents of Machuchal are not enthusiastic about moving to a "better neighborhood." Understandably, they look somewhat askance at kaffee-klatches or neighborhood improvement associations. Machuchalites like Machuchal the way it is and request that those with other preferences go their ways.

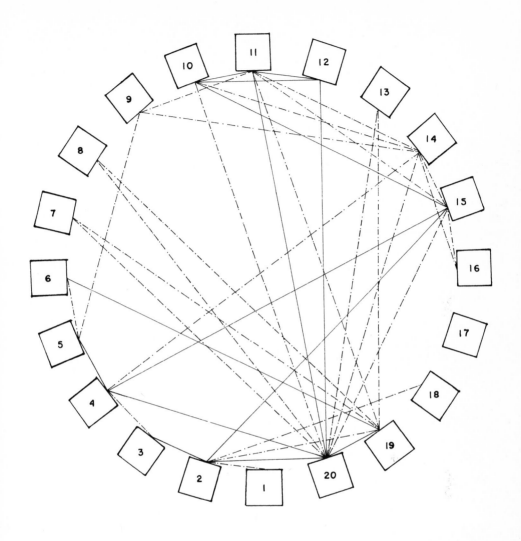

Neighborhood 14—BARRIO MACHUCHAL

		Number
— · — ·	Confirmed (casual) relationships scored 2-3	25
——	Confirmed (intimate) relationships scored 4-5-6	14
	Total	39

Neighborhood 15—BARRIO SEBORUCO

Seboruco is the neighborhood in the sample with the shortest length of residence—an average of fifteen months. Its residents are somewhat lower in socio-economic status than those of Sagrado Corazón. There are about the same number of households without male heads and similar histories of migration. Here, the similarities cease.

Seboruco is located on a just barely reclaimed swamp off Expreso Norte in the eastern part of Santurce. It has few sidewalks and poor street lighting. The streets are paved but there are no sewers, and the odors are strong. It is far from public transportation and shopping facilities. It does not even have easy access to the adjacent expressway. A fence at the end of the street prevents through traffic.

The average household consists of nearly five persons. There are few close neighboring relationships but many casual contacts.

With this combination of poor physical and social conditions it is not surprising that neighborhood satisfaction is low. Only forty percent of the families describe their neighborhood as a good place to live. Many would like to move, but cannot afford housing elsewhere.

One of our respondents has lived in Seboruco for fifty-four years. When he first arrived, there were no public transportation routes and he had to walk several miles to get to the city. This rural isolation was gradually reduced by the growth of Santurce until Seboruco became a lower class neighborhood on the edge of the urban core.

The last decade of relocation and replanning in Santurce has produced considerable instability here. In the face of an insecure future no one appears willing to make social or physical investments in the area. The residents content themselves with friendships outside the neighborhood, and dream about the day they can move.

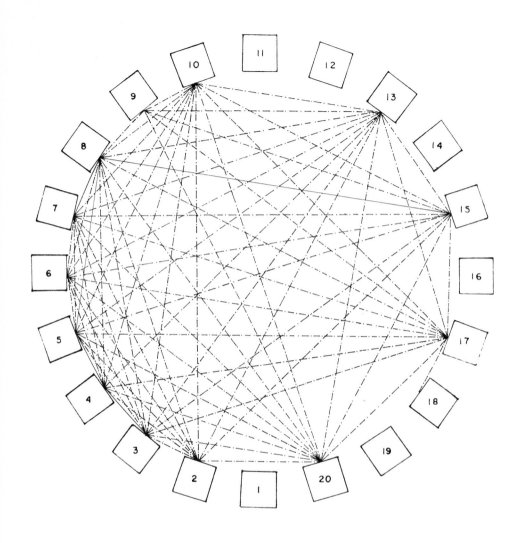

Neighborhood 15 — BARRIO SEBORUCO

		Number
— · — ·	Confirmed (casual) relationships scored 2-3	67
——	Confirmed (intimate) relationships scored 4-5-6	5
	Total	72

Neighborhood 16—BARRIO LOÍZA

In this neighborhood, the houses extend on both sides of the street to the principal intersection in an unbroken pattern. Most of them are cement structures of uniform design. Most of the families are middle-class.

The average household comprises three persons. A surprising number of adult relatives are included. There are few children. Educational attainment approaches the urban average at 7.9 years. Thirty-five percent of the households have no male head. In these cases, the woman is usuallly employed in a minor white collar position. The women of this neighborhood are much older than average, nearly fifty-two. Most of the males are employed in clerical and service occupations scattered throughout Santurce and the satellite cities.

Twenty percent moved to their present address from the same barrio, and the great majority from elsewhere in Santurce. The average length of residence is six years—somewhat below normal.

Although several churches are located nearby, these families do not report much regular attendance. They do take advantage of the convenient shopping facilities on Loíza Street and count this as an advantage of living in the neighborhood.

Loíza is slightly below average in volume of neighboring. It has few intimate relationships. Several families are isolated. There are three incomplete cliques.

Neighborhood satisfaction is high, but the younger families look forward to more upward mobility. Ninety percent describe the neighborhood as "a good place to live." More than half of the families plan to remain here, but slightly more than a third have plans to move to one of the new suburbs.

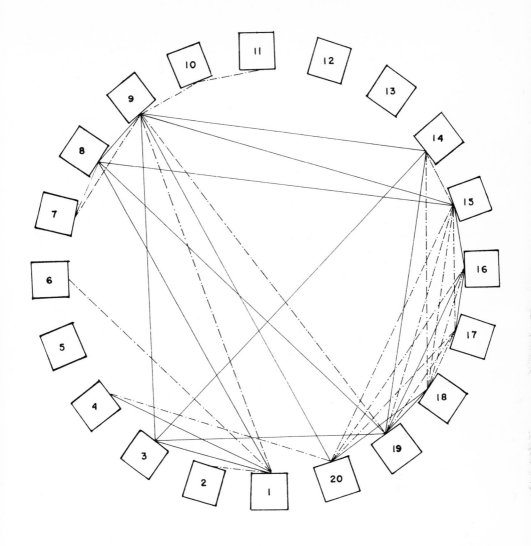

Neighborhood 16 — BARRIO LOÍZA

		Number
— . — . Confirmed (casual) relationships scored 2-3		19
—— Confirmed (intimate) relationships scored 4-5-6		19
	Total	38

Neighborhood 17—BARRIO
MONTEFLORES

Monteflores is perhaps the most representative of our Central Santurce neighborhoods. It contains a mixture of single and multiple dwellings, built from three to forty years ago, and a mixture of upper, middle, and lower class residents. Located on a hill half way between Avenida Ponce de Leon and the Beachfront, the houses command a majestic view of the metropolis.

A small apartment house, into which eight lower and middle class families are crowded, occupies one corner of the site. Across the street stands a single family house built shortly after World War II. A more recent middle-class house stands between the apartment house and a dilapidated hovel. At the opposite end of the same street is an expensive and almost new upper class residence, surrounded by a luxurious garden.

Educational attainment, per capita income, and occupational position cover the range from low to high. Nearly all of the wives, and almost one-half of the husbands were born in rural Puerto Rico. Almost all of them lived at two or more addresses in the Metropolitan Area before coming to Monteflores. They have lived in this neighborhood for an average of six years.

Half of the families are socially isolated and not all of these are the lower class residents. Four additional families maintain only one close neighboring relationship apiece. The remainder form an intimate and self-sufficient clique.

Monteflores' residents seem to approve of this neighboring pattern. The neighbors are described as "helpful," "reasonably cultivated," "quiet," "good," "nice," "moral," and "friendly,"—the neighborhood as "cool," "dry," and in a "convenient location." Not a single respondent expressed a negative opinion of her neighbors or the neighborhood.

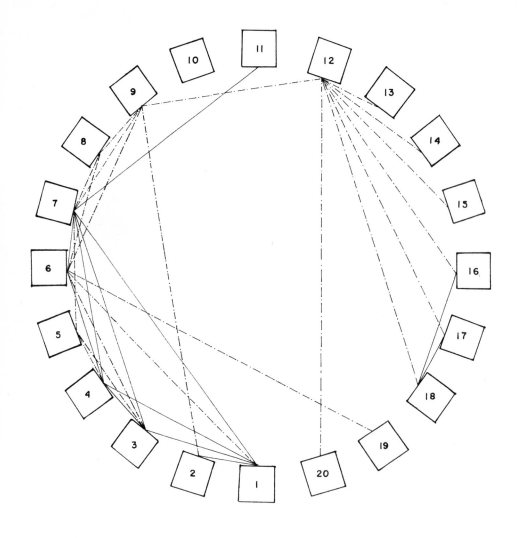

Neighborhood 17 — BARRIO MONTEFLORES

		Number
— · — ·	Confirmed (casual) relationships scored 2-3	20
——	Confirmed (intimate) relationships scored 4-5-6	12
	Total	32

Neighborhood 18—BARRIO VILLA PALMERAS

The area bounded by Avenida Baldorioty de Castro, the San José Lagoon, Eduardo Conde Avenue and Tapia Street is a traditional middle and lower class residential area. Its buildings were constructed during the last stages of expansion of Santurce. Today, it is perhaps the most thoroughly developed part of the Urban Area. Single and multi-family residential units stand side by side on small plots interspersed with many small, commercial establishments. Some of the traditional wooden houses have been replaced by cement structures.

Walking through Villa Palmeras, one feels as if he had been transported back twenty years in the history of the city. The streets are filled with constant activity. Old buildings occupied by bars, businesses, whorehouses and places of recreation are separated by only three or four feet. There are no yards worthy of mention, few sidewalks and scarcely any vegetation.

The residents of Villa Palmeras apparently enjoy their overwhelming lack of privacy. The typical family moved to the district more than eight years ago, a fourth of them from another address in the same barrio and the same number from an adjacent barrio. Several of the wives were born in this part of Santurce.

The average household has four members. There are many children. Forty percent of the households have no male heads. The average educational level of adults is 8.5 years. The average weekly income is less than twenty-five dollars. About a third of the men are employed in the immediate vicinity and an equal number in Old San Juan.

Although the intensity of neighboring is slightly above average, nearly several families are socially isolated and the neighborhood can not be considered an integral unit. Nevertheless, neighborhood satisfaction is fairly high. "The environment is favorable for the future of my daughters." "Although there are too many colored people, it is a good place because it is quiet." "It is a good environment, quiet, and we have never had any trouble with our neighbors."

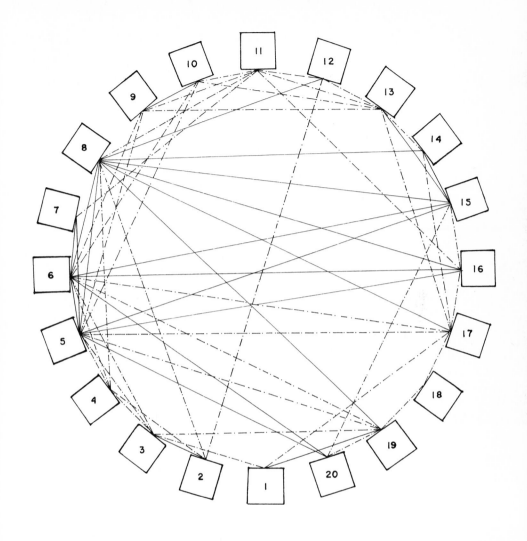

Neighborhood 18—BARRIO VILLA PALMERAS

		Number
—·—· Confirmed (casual) relationships scored 2-3		39
—— Confirmed (intimate) relationships scored 4-5-6		22
	Total	61

In past decades, many wealthy San Juaneros moved their entire households miles to summer homes in Punta Las Marias. Some built beautiful estates overlooking the ocean with patios, terraces, guest and servant quarters. Others constructed less permanent wooden buildings, as bathhouses and picnic headquarters.

World War II brought the Army to the Point, and there was some increase in population. Even at the end of the war, however, it preserved its isolation. The last stop of the trolley was about a mile away.

Clearance of the vast adjacent swamp, road improvement, the departure of the Army, and the arrival of new middle class families, transformed the district. The salesmen, administrators, professionals, and managers who were among the first to benefit from Puerto Rico's economic growth, led this movement. The old residents fled and Punta Las Marias became Proper. All the families in our sample have children, are educated, support culture, participate in civic organizations. All of them are white.

Broad, well-paved streets follow a regular grid pattern. All homes are single family structures of North American style. Old houses have walls and foliage for privacy. New houses have cyclone fences to "keep out the riff-raff." The local neighborhood improvement association has a policy of indiscriminate opposition to all government programs.

Las Marias is just below the average study neighborhood in the volume of neighboring.

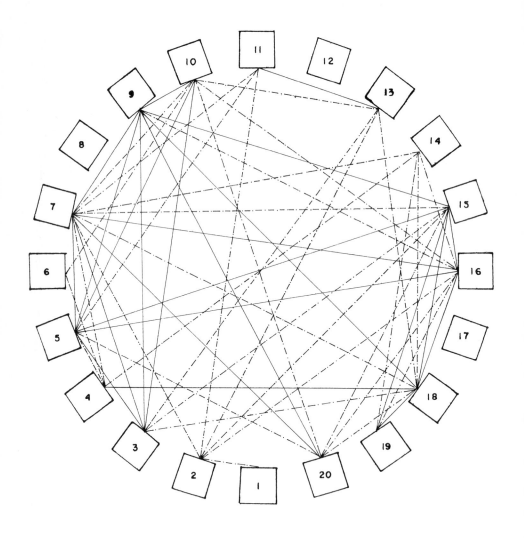

Neighborhood 19—BARRIO LAS MARIAS

		Number
— · — ·	Confirmed (casual) relationships scored 2-3	33
——	Confirmed (intimate) relationships scored 4-5-6	23
	Total	56

Neighborhood 20—BARRIO MERHOFF

Merhoff is an area in the eastern section of Santurce, amazingly isolated. It is a ten to fifteen minute walk from the nearest main avenue (Avenida Barbosa). It is bordered by the Laguna on two sides and by the old racetrack and the road to the Oratorio on the other sides. The district was settled about 1935, absorbing the last waves of migration induced by the depression. As a result of its isolation, it forms a community in a much more significant sense than most urban districts.

The land elevation is fairly high, a desirable feature here. However, there are no paved streets or sidewalks, street lighting is poor and there is no sewage system. Houses are of wood, with cement floors and zinc roofs. There are a few cement block structures, mostly commercial. The houses appear fairly clean, some are newly painted and some are surrounded by fruit trees and plants.

The isolation of Merhoff has stimulated the development of small shops (colmado, farmacia, barbería, zapatería, bazár, cafetín, billár).

The population density is 81 persons per acre. The average household consists of nearly five persons. Educational attainment is low—about five years.

The neighbors in Merhoff are friendly, although they do not visit much. Their houses are so close that they talk or shout to each other from the windows. Regardless of the crowding there is a certain amount of self-imposed privacy—nobody bothers anybody (nadie se mete con nadie). The daytime activities of the women are limited to household duties and an occasional trip to the market. Children play freely in the streets, and visit among the houses.

Thirty percent of the households have no male head. Most of the men are employed on semi-skilled jobs. The per capita income is nine dollars a week. On week-ends, many of the men lounge in the streets, work on their cars, or visit the "billár" and the "cafetín."

The priests of the Oratorio at the entrance to Merhoff often show films, but these are not attended by many residents. Religious feeling is intense here. Although close to a large Catholic center, most of the people are "evangélicos" who do not believe in dancing, drinking, smoking or cosmetics. They constantly criticize Catholics, and this leads to many fights.

Neighborhood satisfaction is fair. They do not like the dust from the cement factory, the unpaved road, or the distance to transportation and public facilities, but they are happy with each other. Half of the families plan to remain in the neighborhood and only one respondent definitely plans to move.

An element of insecurity threatens their isolation. There is talk that the land may be bought up by an "Americano" or that the government will relocate them to make a park. Although there is disagreement about the rumors, some families have their houses up for sale.

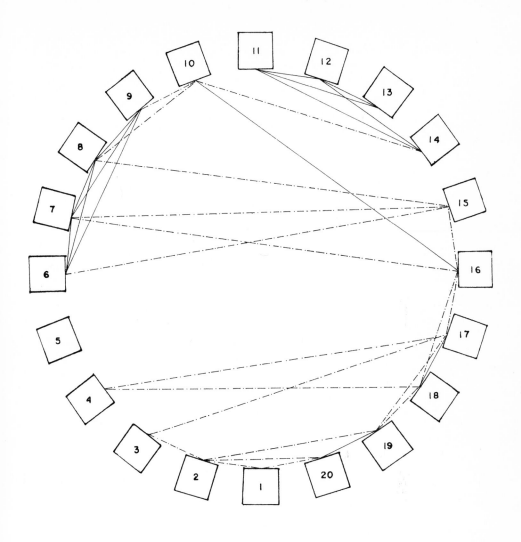

Neighborhood 20 — BARRIO MERHOF

		Number
— · — ·	Confirmed (casual) relationships scored 2-3	20
——	Confirmed (intimate) relationships scored 4-5-6	14
	Total	34

Las Casas has a more pleasant location than the public housing project located in Puerta de Tierra. It stands on a hill overlooking the San José lagoon and enjoys a fine breeze from the sea. When the sewage disposal plant, now under construction, is completed and the odor of the lagoon disappears, the site will be further improved.

Las Casas is convenient to some, but not all, urban facilities. A bus line passes in front of the project, but the journey to work is long. Most parts of the city, however, are accessible. There are supermarkets and other shops within easy walking distance.

Except for the fact that nearly half of the residents are non-white, the Las Casas population closely resembles that of Puerta de Tierra. Education and income are low. The proportion of children is high. In the typical case, both husband and wife were born in rural Puerto Rico. They lived in two other parts of the urban area before moving to the project. In contrast to the pattern we discovered in Puerta de Tierra, only ten percent came to Las Casas from the same barrio.

Socially, the project residents are poorly integrated but most families maintain a single close relationship with a neighbor.

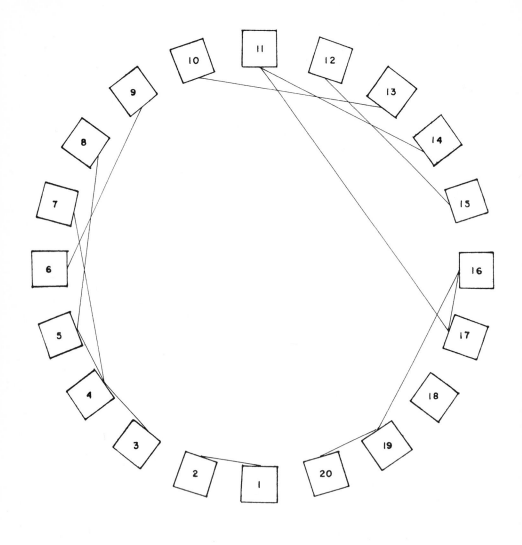

Neighborhood 21 — BARRIO LAS CASAS

		Number
—·—·	Confirmed (casual) relationships scored 2-3	0
——	Confirmed (intimate) relationships scored 4-5-6	13
	Total	13

Neighborhood 22—BARRIO MONACILLO URBANO

Neighborhood Monacillo Urbano was built about 1953. Each house has an acre or so of land, and the roads conform to the contour of the land in keeping with the best principles of modern design. The houses blend with the landscape, and the gardens are elaborately cultivated. Giant picture windows set with ornate lamps adorn the facades. Every house has a variety of cars, television sets, and other objects of conspicuous consumption.

The residents are those who have really made good. Born in rural Puerto Rico, these merchants, managers, and professionals compete with a small minority of Continentals as personifications of the American Dream.

With attache case under arm, the men leave each morning for their "thirty minute" drive to work. After the women have spent an hour or so delivering their children to school, they return to the neighborhood to begin their careful neighboring. Monacillo Urbano is slightly above average in volume of neighboring. No one, however, admits to just a casual relationship with any of her neighbors; nor should one be too intimate. The standard lies somewhere between and all seem to fall in line.

Most of these families planned the construction of their present houses with an architect before moving here from the beachfront. They express a high degree of satisfaction. "Yes, the neighborhood is stupendous, especially because of the spirituality."

Transportation is clearly a problem, but that is a price these families are more than willing to pay for their elegant seclusion.

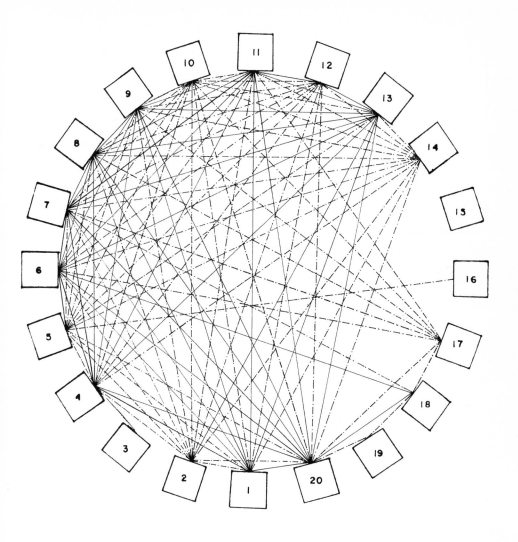

Neighborhood 22 — BARRIO MONACILLO URBAN

		Number
—·—·	Confirmed (casual) relationships scored 2-3	63
——	Confirmed (intimate) relationships scored 4-5-6	42
	Total	105

Neighborhood 23—BARRIO HATO REY SUR

Hato Rey Sur was built about five years later than Hato Rey Central, in 1940. It has broad winding streets, sidewalks, and parkways, lined by single and multiple dwellings.

It lies at the top of a gentle slope. The elevation is sufficient to give the full advantage of the breeze, since the land slopes downward to the west and south. Those who live in the taller buildings enjoy a sweeping view of the new suburbs and the beautiful distant mountains.

These people are not much different from those of Hato Rey Central but they have attained their current socio-economic position at younger ages. Talking to them, one realizes that they are definitely on the way up. They are the middle class counterparts of the residents of Mercado.

This is evident when neighborhood satisfaction is compared with intentions to move. When asked whether this neighborhood was a good place to live, their response was unanimous and enthusiastic. The neighborhood is "clean," "cool," "quiet," "convenient," "independent," "wonderful," "noiseless," "great," "accessible," "private," "magnificent" and "undisturbed." Reading the interviews, one gets the impression that they are prepared to outlast our famous residents of Sagrado Corazón. When asked if they planned to remain here, however, forty percent report plans for migrating to one of the "better" suburbs.

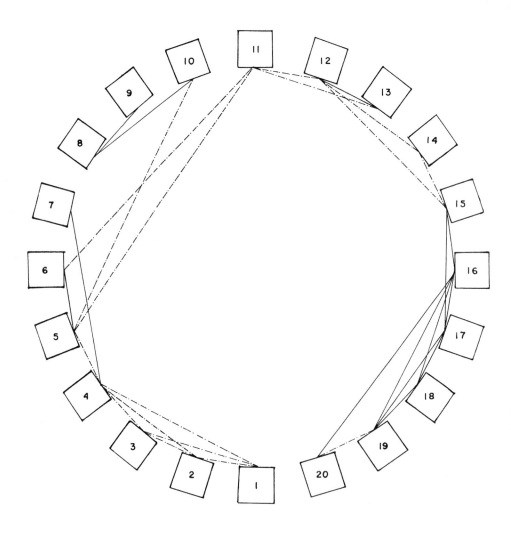

Neighborhood 23 — BARRIO HATO REY SUR

		Number
—·—·	Confirmed (casual) relationships scored 2-3	16
——	Confirmed (intimate) relationships scored 4-5-6	14
	Total	30

Neighborhood 24—BARRIO HATO REY CENTRAL

Hato Rey Central is an upper middle class neighborhood built about 1935. It has a mixture of single and multiple structures. A grade school and a grocery store are the only non-residential buildings in the neighborhood. The houses are far apart, and carefully maintained. The streets are shaded and well-paved. The primary disadvantage of the neighborhood is its distance from public transportation.

Seventy-five percent of the men and sixty percent of the women were born in rural Puerto Rico. The average family moved to this neighborhood from another nearby, about nine years ago. Statistically, there is nothing striking about them, except perhaps that their church attendance is very high.

Hato Rey Central is in the upper fifth of the neighborhoods studied in volume of neighboring. The pattern of interaction is extensive rather than intensive. Everyone knows everyone casually, but there are few close relationships. All of the respondents agree that their neighborhood is an excellent place in all respects except for its lack of public transportation.

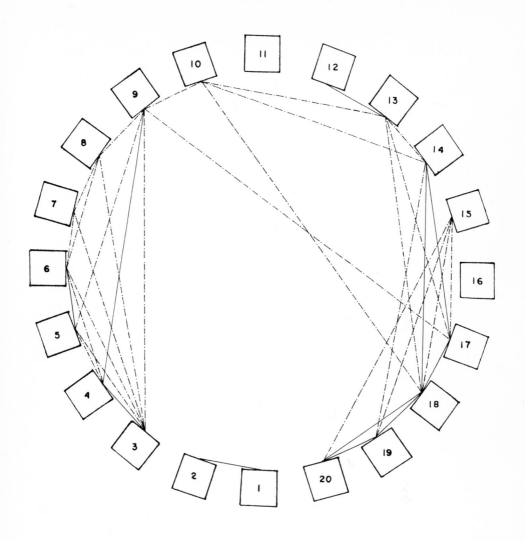

Neighborhood 24—BARRIO HATO REY CENTRAL

		Number
—·—·	Confirmed (casual) relationships scored 2-3	25
——	Confirmed (intimate) relationships scored 4-5-6	11
	Total	36

While most families appreciate proximity to urban services, it is possible to live too close to them as the residents of Pueblo have discovered. This is a barrio immediately adjacent to the old town of Rio Piedras, which was founded in 1714. After World War II, when Rio Piedras began to expand more rapidly, the old residential barrio of Pueblo was invaded by commercial establishments, offices and intense traffic. It is now composed of a mixture of old upper class homes and more recent commercial and apartment buildings.

An upper class style of life is still maintained, although somewhat feebly. Two distinct types of families live in Pueblo. The former are those whose status surpasses their income, mostly teachers connected with the University. The latter are white collar workers. The educators walk to work in Rio Piedras, while the salesman and clerks drive to eastern Santurce. While the white collar workers are newer to the neighborhood, the long residence of the educators raises the average tenure to ten years, the second highest among the twenty-five neighborhoods studied.

The Pueblo neighborhood is well integrated socially, although casual relationships predominate. In expressing their satisfaction with the neighborhood, our respondents make it clear that although the noise and traffic are intolerable during the day, it is quiet and peaceful at night. Thirty-five percent intend to move.

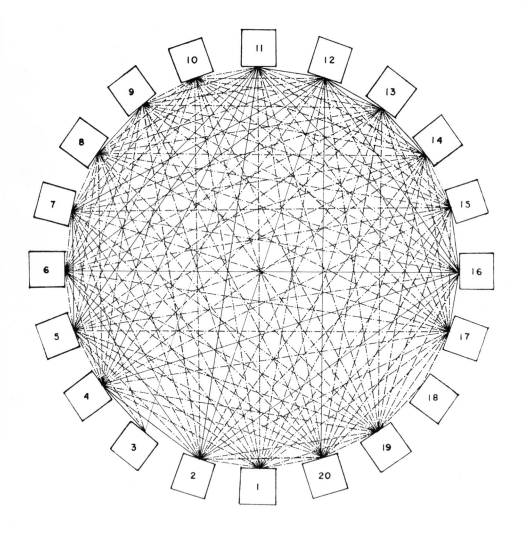

Neighborhood 25 — BARRIO PUEBLO

		Number
— . — .	Confirmed (casual) relationships scored 2-3	133
——	Confirmed (intimate) relationships scored 4-5-6	27
	Total	160

4 The Correlates of Interaction

Using the Neighborhood Data

The data concerning neighboring relationships consist of the responses of 500 women representing 500 families located in twenty-five neighborhoods in the San Juan Urban Area, as measured by the Neighborhood Interaction Scale in 1960.

It will be recalled that the twenty-five neighborhoods were selected by drawing the longest possible straight line linking a pair of points in every odd numbered barrio and taking a predetermined point on the line in the center of the barrio. The nearest intersection was taken as the starting point. Twenty contiguous dwelling units were counted from this intersection along a street running northerly. The neighborhood was *arbitrarily* defined as consisting of twenty dwelling units for the purposes of this study, and is not represented as a "natural area."

Ideally, any measurement of interaction ought to combine at least two dimensions—extensity and intensity. In this case, extensity is defined as the number of neighbors known, and intensity as the average intimacy with which they are known. Because of the arbitrary standardization of neighborhood size, it is clear that the measure of extensity has an intrinsic defect, in that a family's location in the neighborhood territory influences its opportunity to reveal the full extent of its relationships. A family located in the middle of the area has roughly twice the opportunity to be mentioned by its neighbors as one on the fringe. This defect was foreseen when the method of selecting the sample was adopted, but it was accepted as part of the cost of obtaining a full matrix of interaction for groups of standard size with each relationship confirmed by both participants.[1]

Some of the measures described previously, like the Interaction Outscore, are unsuitable as measures of an individual family's tendency to interact with its neighbors, because they are distorted by differential opportunities to report the full range of relationships. Only *mean* scores—in which this distortion is minimized although not entirely removed—will be used for this purpose.

Of the various mean scores calculated, Intensity of Neighboring is the most interesting. This score is the sum of the confirmed scale values of a family's neighboring relationships, divided by the number of relationships.

A confirmed score, based on the response of both "members" of the relationship has obvious advantages over the corresponding unconfirmed scores, since it is less affected by the errors and biases inherent in anyone's observation of his own behavior.

It should be repeated once more that the study was designed to obtain confirmed neighboring scores and that the arbitrary definition of the neighborhood as twenty contiguous dwelling units was adopted to make possible the charting of neighborhood relationships on the basis of information from both participants in each relationship. As the result of this design, we have the responses of each of the families studied with respect to each of nineteen other families, and also the responses of the nineteen other families with

[1] It is also possible that the volume of interaction in a neighborhood is affected by the absolute number of accessible families. For a demonstration of such an effect in larger communities, see Stuart C. Dodd, "A Power of Town Size Predicts an Internal Interacting," *Social Forces*, Vol. 36, December 1957.

respect to the subject. Thus the confirmed score is based on the *minimum* degree of intimacy upon which a pair of neighboring families agree. It is highly probable that if Family X says that it associates with Family Y at a level of 4, and Family Y says it associates with Family X on a level of 2, the "true" degree of intimacy is not less than 2.

The Distribution of Intensity Scores

Thus far, we have introduced the scale used to elicit neighboring data from our respondents, described the measurements of neighboring this scale permits, and explained why our major analysis of neighboring will be pursued by means of the Intensity score. Before presenting the findings about correlates of neighboring, a glance at the distribution of Intensity scores in this sample is advisable.

Intensity scores range from a low of zero to a high of 6.00. The mean of this distribution is 2.40, representing a level of neighboring about midway between "stop and talk with them regularly (only one adult from each family involved)" and "stop and talk with them regularly (all adults involved)."

Sixteen of our subject families have scores of zero. Ten of these are complete isolates who do not know the names or faces of any of their neighbors and are not known by name or face to any of their neighbors. The other six families either fail to confirm others' reports with reference to themselves or report relationships not confirmed by their neighbors.

At the other end of the distribution, there are sixteen families whose Intensity score is 6.00. These families sustain confirmed relationships involving "mutual visiting and entertaining in each other's houses, including drinking or dining" with every family they know within their neighborhoods.

The modal Intensity score is 1.00. There are forty-four families at this level. The standard deviation of the distribution is 1.16, so that it is skewed to the right.

The median Intensity score is 2.20. Scores 0.00 to 1.59 fall into the first quartile, scores 1.60 to 2.19 into the second, scores 2.20 to 3.09 into the third, and scores 3.10 to 6.00 into the fourth quartile.

These figures probably overstate the level of neighboring in San Juan. As we will later show, intensity of neighboring is positively correlated with income, occupational status, and education. Since the upper levels of the socio-economic pyramid are overrepresented in our sample, there is probably some upward distortion in the averages.

Is this a high, low, or moderate amount of neighboring for a city like San Juan? How does the intensity of neighboring compare with North American cities? No adequate answers can be given to these questions without comparable data. Still, it seems worthwhile to examine the available information for clues.

Earlier studies using the Neighborhood Interaction Scale provide a few points of reference. In the pilot study of 134 non-selected neighborhoods in Minneapolis and St. Paul, which contributed to the development of the scale, the mean intensity of neighboring (with ten closest neighbors) was 1.47.[2] This figure represents a level of neighboring barely above a casual greeting relationship. For comparative purposes, it should be noted this mean (a) is not based on confirmed scores, as in San Juan; (b) refers to a subject family's ten closest neighbors; (c) includes all ten neighbors in its base. These points have diverse consequences: Intensity is *higher* than it would have been had confirmed scores been used and had the neighborhood been defined to include twenty contiguous households as in the present study, and *lower* than it would have been had the number of *relationships* been used as the base of the mean.

A series of studies applied the Neighborhood Interaction Scale to University Village in Minneapolis. While confirmed neighboring scores were not investigated directly, they can be computed from data presented in two of these studies. When this is done, average Intensity scores of 2.63 and 2.87 are obtained from the Shimota and Cole[3] studies, respectively.

Once again the comparison with other data—although imperfect—indicates that the absolute level of neighboring in San Juan is high. The University Village neighborhood studied by Shimota and Cole was extraordinarily homogeneous. All family heads had the same occupation of student,

[2] Caplow and Forman, *op. cit.*, p. 360.
[3] Kenneth L. Shimota, *op. cit.*
   Thomas D. Cole, *op. cit.*

all were white, veterans, married, with small children, approximately of the same age, and with approximately the same resources. They lived in identical units with nearly identical furniture. The length of occupancy was standardized. Their isolation from other neighborhoods was almost complete and they consciously visualized themselves as being "all together in the same boat." Everything in the special situation of the University Villagers facilitated an unusually high—almost abnormal—intensity of neighboring. Yet the average intensity is almost as high for our cross-section of San Juan residents and in some neighborhoods, much higher.

Smith, Form and Stone[4] developed a Guttman Scale to measure neighborhood social intimacy in the metropolitan area of Lansing, Michigan, using a randomly selected twenty percent (N = 116) of their total sample. The scale contained four items: (a) How well do you think the people in the neighborhood know each other? (b) About how many of them would you say you know by name? (c) About how many do you spend a whole afternoon or evening with every now and then? (d) If you had your choice would you continue living in this neighborhood? The lowest scale score was characterized by the following responses to these four questions: (a) not at all, not so well; (b) none, a few; (c) none; (d) no, don't know. Eighteen percent of the sample from which this scale was derived fell into this lowest scale category. These are roughly comparable to the 3.2% of the San Juan sample having zero intensity scores. Axelrod[5] using data obtained from an area sample of Detroit, (N = 749), reports that fifty percent of his respondents associate with neighbors less frequently than once a month.

Bell and Boat,[6] studying male residents in four San Francisco census tracts of varying occupational and family composition, found that about forty-five percent of their subjects (N = 701) were "never" involved in neighborhood participation. The majority of those reporting neighborhood participation said that their associations with neighbors usually occurred at home. Although these results cannot be compared

[4] Joel Smith, William H. Form and Gregory P. Stone, "Local Intimacy in a Middle-Sized City," American Journal of Sociology, Vol. 60, November 1954, pp. 276-284.
[5] Morris Axelrod, "Urban Structure and Social Participation," American Sociological Review, Vol. 21, February 1956.
[6] Wendell Bell and Marion D. Boat, "Urban Neighborhoods and Informal Social Relations," American Journal of Sociology, Vol. 62, January 1957.

directly to ours, they suggest a very different pattern of neighboring.

Greer and Kube[7] used a neighboring scale developed by Wallin in their study of women's neighborliness in four Los Angeles areas. Their item of "no neighboring" seems to be equivalent to our item "do not know their names or faces." If this is correct, then 20.7 percent of their subjects (N = 611) report "no neighboring," compared to 3.2 percent of the San Juan respondents.

The question with which we started this discussion cannot be answered precisely, but these straws in the wind suggest that neighboring may be more intense in San Juan than in urban areas of the United States.

In this chapter, we shall try to discover whether the *intensity* of a family's neighborhood relationships is related to its other characteristics. We want to know, for example, whether the age and occupation of the family head and the presence or absence of children, influence the family's willingness or ability to associate with neighbors.

We shall be curious about whether the type of housing, the amount of disposable income, or the length of residence at a given address, show any statistical association with neighboring. If we do find consistent regularities in the data, we shall want to see whether they can be explained.

In examining our neighboring interaction data for regularities, we have typically used two measures: the chi-square statistic as a test of independence, and gamma (γ) as an index of assocation.

The former answers the question: what is the probability that two sets of variables distribute independently, so that the pattern into which the cases fall can be accounted for by chance. If the probability is very low (less than .05), we reject the hypothesis of statistical independence and permit ourselves the inference that, in one way or another, the two variables depend upon one another.

This established, we want to know more about the degree and direction of association. Several measures of association are available. Each has advantages and disadvantages. Of those considered as appropriate for these data, we have chosen *gamma* for a number of reasons: (1) as a single index, it is not restricted to 2 × 2 tables, (2) it is not a merely redundant function of chi-square, (3) its size is not

[7] Scott Greer and Ella Kube, *Urban Worlds*, unpublished manuscript, 1955.

restricted either by the number of cells in a table or the distribution of marginals, (4) it is easy to read and interpret.

The other measures considered were C and ϕ^2, both more familiar and more conventional than gamma. ϕ^2 is a simple function of chi-square, and in this sense redundant. It is limited to 2×2 tables. It can reach its maximum only when the marginal distributions of the variables are identical—a condition not frequently met in our data.

C can be computed for tables of varying size. Its value is dependent upon table size (for example, the maximum C obtainable in a 2×2 table is .707); it can reach this maximum only under the condition of identical marginal distributions, and it is also a function of chi-square.

Gamma, introduced by Goodman and Kruskal[8], measures the probability of obtaining like or unlike ordering in cross classification tables, conditional on the absence of ties. Its range is from 1.00, indicating a total predominance of like ordering, to — 1.00 indicating a total predominance of unlike ordering. Suppose two individuals, each classified on two ordered variables, A and B, to be drawn independently and randomly from a population. If the two cases are "tied," i.e., if either the A values of the two individuals or their B values are the same, the cases are ignored. If ties aside, there is a positive association between the two variables A and B, we expect that if A_1 is greater than A_2, given positive association, B_1 will be greater than B_2. If there is negative association, ties aside, we expect the order of A's be reversed in the order of B's (if A_1 is greater than A_2, B_1 is less than B_2). Gamma gives us a direct measure of the probability of such association. For example, the gamma of .53 found for Table 1 of the appendix to Chapter Four means that there is a 53 percent greater probability of getting like than unlike ordering of intensity of neighboring and quality of housing when pairs of cases are drawn independently and randomly from this population.

Three additional points should be noted about gamma. (1) It assumes "ordered" data, produced, for example, by ordinal scales. Most of our data is clearly of this sort. In a few other cases, it does not strain the imagination to perceive the classes as ordered—for example, a white-nonwhite pair of classes is ordered on a status continuum. In the few instances where the data classes do not seem to be ordered, we have not

[8] Leo A. Goodman and William H. Kruskal, "Measures of Association for Cross-Classifications," *Journal of the American Statistical Association*, Vol. 49, December 1954, pp. 732-764.

computed gamma. (2) Gamma is zero not only in the case of statistical independence—but for some types of curvilinear relationship between variables. Since, in such cases, gamma does not provide an adequate description of the distributions, we do not present it. (3) In the case of a 2 × 2 table, gamma is identical with Yule's familiar Q.

For convenience, the correlates of the Intensity score are presented under five headings:

1. Housing characteristics
2. Stratification characteristics
3. Locational characteristics
4. Demographic characteristics
5. Attitudinal characteristics

Housing Characteristics

Prior to the interviewing phase of the project, the quality of each dwelling unit in the sample was rated by two of the authors after identifying the following characteristics:

Housing type	Private or public
Age of building	Year constructed
Structure type	Single or multiple dwelling
Area development	Fully developed or partly developed
Homogeneity	Homogeneous or heterogeneous
Function	Purely residential or partly non-residential
Available facilities	Presence and absence of paving, sidewalks, street lighting, etc.

Using these seven items, and assuming that San Juaneros prefer:

private to public housing,
new to old construction,
single to multiple dwellings,
developed to underdeveloped areas,
residential to non-residential blocks,
the presence of public services to their absence,

each dwelling unit in the sample was placed in one of eight *housing levels*. They range down from AA, which would be the rating, for example, of a newly constructed mansion in one of the exclusive Beach Front developments, to DD, which might be the rating of a badly weathered shack in one of the squalid slums along the lagoon.

HOUSING LEVEL: Table 1 shows the association between intensity of neighboring and housing level, as measured by the gamma coefficient and the chi-square formula. The relationship is positive and significant. In other words, a family in our sample whose home rates "high" (AA to BB) is likely to have closer neighboring relationships than a family whose home rates low (CC to DD). The correlation also appears to hold when the sample is broken down into finer categories.[9]

BEDROOM DENSITY: A simpler measure of housing quality is bedroom density; the arithmetic ratio of the number of persons living in a dwelling unit to the number of sleeping rooms in that unit. Ratios of 1.5 persons per bedroom or less are classified as uncrowded. Ratios of more than 1.5 are classified as crowded. Table 2 shows that bedroom density is inversely and significantly associated with neighboring.

IMPROVEMENTS: Each neighborhood included in this study was rated on a series of items having to do with available public services and amenities. This *Improvements Index* takes account of street cleaning, sidewalks, paving, street lighting, sewers, public transportation, noise, offensive odors, shopping facilities and automobile traffic. The association of the Improvements Index with the neighboring score is shown in Table 3. The two measures are positively and significantly associated.

HOMOGENEITY: Previous studies of neighborhood interaction have shown greater intensity of interaction in homogeneous neighborhoods. The data presented in Table 4 confirm this expectation. There is a positive and significant association between homogeneity and intensity of neighboring.

A neighborhood was classified as homogeneous if all of its dwelling units fell within three contiguous housing levels. This is only one of several types of neighborhood homogeneity. Homogeneity can also be measured with respect to such characteristics as income, occupation, education, origins, length of tenure, number of children, and age. The reason

[9] As a procedural check, the direction of the difference within dichotomous classifications was examined for all the variables discussed in this chapter and correlations are not ordinarily presented as significant unless the direction of the differences *within* the halves of the major dichotomous classification is consistent with the difference noted on the chi-square table.

we have not made more use of these other measurements of homogeneity is that, compared to the total range of urban neighborhoods studied with the Neighborhood Interaction Scale, all of the neighborhoods in this sample are rather heterogeneous.

There is no single neighborhood in which a majority of household heads fall in the same age group, the same educational level, the same occupational category, or the same income bracket. Neighborhoods in North American cities and suburbs are often homogeneous in all these respects. There may be such neighborhoods in San Juan also, but not in this sample.

Somewhat to our surprise, certain salient features of the family dwelling do *not* seem to be related to intensity of neighboring. No differences were found between public and private housing units, between owned and rented homes, or even between single-family and multiple structures.

Stratification Characteristics

Some of the characteristics already discussed are essentially attributes of stratification. Housing quality, amenities, and bedroom density have obvious economic implications although some families in a given stratum may devote more or less of their resources to housing than other families in the same stratum.

All of the socio-economic indicators to be discussed in this section are interrelated. Indeed, the attributes of stratification in a local population *must* be related.[10] Nevertheless, for the sake of clarity, they are presented and discussed separately.

OCCUPATION: On the basis of information obtained during the interview, the Dictionary of Occupational Titles was used to classify the occupation of the head of household into one of the following categories: professional; semi-professional; managerial and official; clerical and kindred; sales and

[10] For evidence on this point, see Wendell Bell, "Social Areas: Typology of Urban Neighborhoods" in Marvin B. Sussman (ed.), *Community Structure and Analysis*, New York, Thomas Y. Crowell, 1959, pp. 61-92; and Theodore R. Anderson and Lee L. Bean, "The Shevkv-Bell Social Areas: Confirmation of Results and a Re-interpretation," *Social Forces*, Vol. 40, December 1961.

kindred; service; skilled; semi-skilled; and unskilled. Not fall-ing into this scheme, and classified separately, were operators of small businesses, renters and investors, public welfare re-cipients, the unemployed, the retired, and the ill. The find-ings are summarized in Table 5.[11] Intensity of neighboring is positively associated with occupational prestige.

EDUCATION: The educational level of each family in the sample was represented by the years of education achieved by husband and wife, or by the wife alone in families with-out male heads. The conventional coding was used. The number 8 represents graduation from grade school, 12 repre-sents the completion of high school, and 19 is the maximum score for professional or graduate education. When husband and wife differ in achieved educational level, an average is taken to represent the family. The relationship between edu-cational level and intensity of neighboring score is positive and clearly significant. [Table 6] People with education be-yond the high school level are more likely to associate with their neighbors, regardless—so far as we can tell—of the neighbors' educational level.[12]

INCOME: Tables 7 and 8 show the association between in-come and intensity of neighboring. Table 7 is based on the family's total weekly income, including the earnings of all wage earners and any other income received. Table 8 is based on *per capita* weekly income. The data are incomplete, since information about income could not be obtained in 75 cases. Nevertheless, the relationship between income and in-tensity of neighboring score is clearly significant. Families with higher incomes tend to know their neighbors better.

Locational Characteristics

MOBILITY: There seems to be very little relationship be-tween a family's past mobility, and its propensity to neigh-

[11] The "high" cell includes proprietors, professionals and semi-profes-sionals, clerical and sales personnel and those living on investments. The "low" cell includes service, skilled, semi-skilled and unskilled workers, relief clients and the unemployed. Retired and disabled workers are not included in the analysis. The table combines male and female heads of households. The results for each of them taken separately are consistent with Table 5.

[12] See Chapter Six.

boring. No relationship was found between the intensity of neighboring and the birthplace of the family head, the time elapsed since migration to San Juan, the distance from previous address, or the number of previous addresses. There was a small but statistically significant relationship between intensity of neighboring and the length of the principal breadwinner's journey to work. High neighboring scores are associated with short journeys to work.

RESIDENCE IN SANTURCE: There is a puzzling relationship between residence in Santurce and neighboring scores. Families whose *present* address is in Sancturce, and families in which either the husband's or wife's *previous* address was in Santurce, show significantly lower intensities of neighboring, as may be seen in Tables 9 and 10.[13]

The explanation for this finding may be that all but one of the neighborhoods characterized as heterogeneous (on the index previously described) are located in Santurce. Table 11 compares neighboring scores in homogeneous and heterogeneous neighborhoods, all in Santurce. The differences are significant.

DURATION OF RESIDENCE: The relationship between duration of residence at the family's present address and the intensity of neighboring is intricate but consistent with what was anticipated from previous neighboring research.[14] If we compare those families who have lived in their present homes for a year or less with the remainder of the sample population, there is a highly significant difference in favor of the families with more "seniority." [Table 12] However, if we ignore the category of newcomers—they constitute about fourteen percent of the sample—and consider only those families who have lived at their present addresses for more than twelve months, we find no relationship at all between duration of residence and intensity of neighboring.[15]

It would appear, that some minimal time is required to establish the pattern of informal relationships within a neighborhood, but that once past the initiation period, a family's

---

[13] Only the data for wife's previous residence is shown.
[14] See especially the three University Village Studies.

[15] Household Tenure

	Intensity of Neighboring	
	High (N)	Low (N)
13-60 mos.	86	76
61-120 mos.	67	57
121-180 mos.	25	22
181-240 mos.	22	16
241 mos.-over	86	76

involvement with its neighbors is as likely to decrease as to increase over time.

Demographic Characteristics

COLOR: During the interview, each respondent was classified on the basis of her skin color, as white, light mulatto, dark mulatto, or Negro. The association between color and intensity of neighboring is shown in Table 13. Those respondents judged to be white are more likely to have high intensity scores than those judged to be non-white. Differences in neighboring among the three non-white categories are non-significant, but this may be because the numbers involved are very small.

AGE: There is a curvilinear relationship between the housewife's age and neighborhood interaction. The families of women between 30 and 59 are more frequently found in the high score category than those of older or younger women. This observation is supported by the data in Table 14. The trend of the data for husband's ages is in the same direction, but not statistically significant.

FAMILY COMPOSITION: No relationship at all was discovered between neighboring score and household size, number of adults, or number of children in the household. The composition of the household is another matter. All of the households in the study were identified as complete or incomplete and as closed or open. A household is *complete* when it includes the three major positions of the nuclear family—husband, wife, child; all others are *incomplete*. A household is *closed* when it includes only the nuclear family positions; it is *open* when it includes persons who are not related to the head as wife or child.

Neither the complete-incomplete nor the closed-open dimension shows much relationship to intensity of neighboring, taken by itself. However, when we compare incomplete and closed households with complete and open households the former show higher neighboring scores. [Table 16] This suggests that a household which contains a nuclear family surrounded by dependents is more self-sufficient and less dependent upon neighbors. This conclusion runs contrary to the general drift of the data, and the consistent association between socially favored characteristics and intensity of neighboring.

Attitudinal Characteristics

RELIGIOSITY: We find no relationship between religious affiliation (or its absence) and intensity of neighboring. However, those who report regular church *attendance* are more likely to have high neighboring scores than those whose church attendance is sporadic or infrequent. [Table 16]

NEIGHBORHOOD SATISFACTION: The interview provides two measures of residents' satisfaction with their neighborhoods. The first is obtained by coding responses to the question, "Do you consider this neighborhood of yours a good place to live?" on a four-point scale. The other is based on a similar coding of responses to the question, "Do you intend to remain in this neighborhood permanently?" Families with high neighboring scores are more likely to evaluate their neighborhoods favorably than those with low neighboring scores [Table 17] and more often plan to stay where they are [Table 18]. The differences, while distinct, are less significant than some of those previously observed, perhaps because a high proportion of all respondents rate their neighborhoods favorably. We shall have more to say about this in a later chapter.

Since neighborhood satisfaction is probably influenced by the quality of the family's own dwelling, which in turn is closely linked with the neighboring score, the relationship between neighborhood satisfaction and intensity of neighboring may be a statistical artifact. This doubt is partially resolved by examining the relationship between neighborhood satisfaction and intensity of neighboring separately for high, middle, and low levels of housing quality. When this is done, the trend of the data is consistently in the same direction as in Table 17, although statistical significance is lost. Similar results are obtained when we attempt to correct the relationship between neighborhood satisfaction and neigh-

boring scores by controlling for the presence of improvements and amenities.

Summary and Conclusions

Let us briefly recapitulate the findings reported in this
chapter. The neighborhood is a system of *voluntary* participation, in contrast to the organized group where participation
is structured by means of membership positions and pre-
defined roles. Based on other studies of sociability,[16] there
seems to be a "universal" correlation between the propensity
to voluntary interaction and favorable social characteristics.
Thus, in this study, the families with more intense neighboring relationships have such varied sources of security as good
education, high income, the "right" color, and comfortable
homes. In the most probable cases, they have lived in their
neighborhood for some time, the wife is middle-aged; they
are above average in church attendance and other kinds of
social participation.

On the other hand, intensity of neighboring does not
seem to be related to other factors suggested by common
sense. If we were able to report that people associate more
closely with their neighbors the longer they live in a neighborhood or that home owners are more likely to show high
neighboring scores than renters or that neighboring is largely
a function of the number of children within the family, the
critics of sociology would be quick to point out that research
of this kind is merely an elaboration of the obvious.

We stress with some diffidence that although a considerable number of characteristics are significantly related to
intensity of neighboring in this body of data, the list of
unrelated (although "obvious") characteristics is even longer.
It includes rental status, home ownership, housing type, birthplace, migration experience, previous mobility, religious affiliation, family size, and number of children.

[16] Supporting evidence expressed in various ways is abundantly available
in any textbook of social psychology. See for example, Gardner Lindzey,
Handbook of Social Psychology, Cambridge, Mass., Addison Wesley,
1954.

The Urban Ambience

The implications of these findings for planning are clear. There are two ways to develop networks of neighboring that are intimate, well-integrated, and satisfying to the participants. Neither way has much to do with architectural design. The result may be achieved by raising the socioeconomic level of the population, and it will also follow from an improvement in housing quality, especially the reduction of crowding. The two usually go hand in hand. Uniformity of housing quality is also favorable but the type of housing, the terms on which it is occupied, and the presence or absence of non-residential functions make very little difference. The planner is excused, so to speak, from planning the social details of good neighborhoods. We need only provide adequate physical facilities, both inside and outside the individual dwelling, and the society need only provide a rising level of welfare, for increased neighborliness to follow of itself.

APPENDIX

The Correlates of Neighboring

TABLE 1

Intensity of Neighboring by Quality of Housing

		Intensity	
		High	Low
Quality of Housing	High	161	90
	Low	88	161

$$X^2 = 41.47, df = 1, p < .001$$
$$\gamma = .53$$

TABLE 2

Intensity of Neighboring by Bedroom Density

		Intensity	
		High	Low
Bedroom Density	Uncrowded	160	123
	Crowded	89	126

$$X^2 = 11.20, df = 1, p < .001$$
$$\gamma = .30$$

TABLE 3

Intensity of Neighboring by Improvements Index

		Intensity	
		High	Low
Neighborhood Improvements	High	180	140
	Low	69	111

$$X^2 = 14.79, df = 1, p < .001$$
$$\gamma = .35$$

TABLE 4

Intensity of Neighboring by Homogeneity Index

	Intensity	
	High	Low
Homogeneous Neighborhoods	152	88
Heterogeneous Neighborhoods	97	163

$X^2 = 33.81$, df $= 1$, p $< .001$

$\gamma = .49$

TABLE 5

Intensity of Neighboring
by Occupation of Head of Household

		Intensity	
		High	Low
*Occupation of Head of Household**	High	171	129
	Low	73	120

$X^2 = 17.28$, df $= 1$, p. $< .001$

$\gamma = .37$

* "High" includes proprietors, professionals and semi-professionals, clerical and sales personnel and those living on investments. "Low" includes service, skilled, semi-skilled and unskilled workers, relief clients and the unemployed.

TABLE 6

Intensity of Neighboring by Educational Level

		Intensity	
		High	Low
*Educational Level**	High	129	80
	Low	117	169

$X^2 = 20.92$, df $= 1$, p $< .001$

$\gamma = .40$

* Mean school grade completed, husband and wife.

TABLE 7

Intensity of Neighboring by Total
Weekly Family Income

		Intensity	
		High	Low
Total Weekly	$120-over	104	56
*Family Income**	$40-$119	90	84
	$39-under	28	63

$$X^2 = 27.27, df = 2, p < .001$$
$$\gamma = .40$$

* Earnings plus unearned income, all family members.

TABLE 8

Intensity of Neighboring by Per Capita Weekly Income

		Intensity	
		High	Low
Per Capita	$40-over	75	53
*Income**	$20-$39	75	37
	$19-under	72	113

$$X^2 = 24.96, df = 2, p < .001$$
$$\gamma = .31$$

* Total income divided by number of family members.

TABLE 9

Intensity of Neighboring by Location of Neighborhood

		Intensity	
		High	Low
Location of Neighborhood	San Juan and Rio Piedras	99	41
	Santurce	150	210

$$X^2 = 34.02, df = 1, p. < .001$$
$$\gamma = .54$$

TABLE 10

Intensity of Neighboring by Wife's Previous Address

	Intensity	
	High	Low
Other than Santurce	136	107
Wife's Previous Address		
Santurce	113	143

$X^2 = 6.97$, df $= 1$, p $< .01$
$\gamma = .23$

TABLE 11

Intensity of Neighboring by Homogeneity Index,
Santurce Neighborhoods Only

	Intensity	
	High	Low
Homogeneous Neighborhoods	64	56
Heterogeneous Neighborhoods	86	154

$X^2 = 10.08$, df $= 1$, p $< .01$
$\gamma = .34$

TABLE 12

Intensity of Neighboring by Household Tenure

	Intensity	
	High	Low
0-12 months	22	52
Household Tenure		
13 months-over	227	197

$X^2 = 14.28$, df $= 1$, p $< .001$
$\gamma = -.46$

TABLE 13

Intensity of Neighboring by Wife's Color

		Intensity	
		High	Low
Wife's Color	White	213	181
	Non-white	36	68

$X^2 = 12.44$, df $= 1$, p $< .001$
$\gamma = .38$

TABLE 14

Intensity of Neighboring by Wife's Age

	Intensity	
	High	Low
Wife's Age*		
20-under	34	49
30-59	175	149
60-over	40	52

$X^2 = 6.36$, df $= 2$, p $< .05$

* Age of female head of household or wife of male head to nearest birthday.

TABLE 15

Intensity of Neighboring by Household Pattern

		Intensity	
		High	Low
Household Pattern	"Incomplete-closed"	48	32
	"Complete-open"	48	61

$X^2 = 4.70$, df $= 1$, p $< .05$
$\gamma = .31$

TABLE 16

Intensity of Neighboring by Church Attendance

		Intensity	
		High	Low
	Regular	126	102
Church Attendance			
	Occasional or less frequent attendance	122	146

$$X^2 = 4.68, df = 1, p < .05$$
$$\gamma = .19$$

TABLE 17

Intensity of Neighboring by Evaluations of Neighborhood

		Intensity	
		High	Low
	Good	185	158
Neighborhood Evaluations			
	Poor-Fair	64	89

$$X^2 = 6.20, df = 1, p < .02$$
$$\gamma = .24$$

TABLE 18

Intensity of Neighboring by Moving Intention

		Intensity	
		High	Low
	Move	85	111
Moving Intention			
	Stay	164	138

$$X^2 = 5.69, df = 1, p < .02$$
$$\gamma = -.22$$

5 Dimensions of Neighboring

Intensity and Extensity

This chapter is concerned with the interdependence of the two fundamental dimensions of any ambience—intensity and extensity.

By intensity, we mean the intimacy of the relationships in which a subject is involved in a given situation during a given interval. The intensity score whose correlates were discussed in the previous chapter is such a measure. It was defined as the sum of the scale values of a family's confirmed relationships within the sample neighborhood, on the Neighborhood Interaction Scale, divided by the number of relationships. Since the Neighborhood Interaction Scale is calibrated in degrees of intimacy, this average is a direct measure of intimacy in this ambience.

By extensity, we mean the number of people with whom

a subject interacts in a given situation during a given interval. We shall use a measure we call ambience size to measure extensity of neighboring in the neighborhoods of San Juan. Let us explore this measure a bit more so that the evidence will be easy to follow. Many of us are not used to visualizing matrices and networks, and it is often difficult to keep in mind the meaning of statistics that describe the interwoven relationships of any sizeable human group.

An ambience is always defined in reference to a subject who interacts with others, and a setting in which that interaction takes place. The setting in this study is always the neighborhood. The subjects are five hundred families distributed into twenty-five neighborhoods, each composed of twenty contiguous dwelling units. Each family has the opportunity of contact with the people who inhabit the nineteen nearby homes. Each family, except for a very small number of isolates, exhibits a pattern of stable relationships with *some* of the families surrounding it. These other families constitute its neighboring ambience. There may be from one to nineteen of them. This is what we mean by ambience size or *extensity* of neighboring. The average intensity of the relationship—as we know—ranges from a scale value of 1, the most casual relationship, to a scale value of 6, which implies very intimate association.

To analyze the interdependence of intensity and extensity of neighboring, we can plot individual cases on a scatter diagram and then group them into tables using average values.

We are going to consider several ambience sizes, sometimes counting all recorded relationships (the total ambience), sometimes counting only relationships involving common activities[1] (the active ambience), or only those involving really close association[2] (the intimate ambience). In all circumstances, however, the analysis will be limited to confirmed relationships—those reported by both participants.

To avoid excessive manipulation of these somewhat esoteric figures, we shall limit attention to a small number of tabulations which display the mutual influence of intensity and extensity. Before examining these tabulations, it may be useful to explain what we are trying to find and why it is important.

The urban way of life involves association with a greater number of people than the rural or village way of life. It has

[1] Scale values of 2 or more.
[2] Scale values of 4 or more.

often been surmised, but seldom demonstrated, that the extensity of the city dweller's interaction implies low intensity. In other words, it is supposed that he who knows many people can not know any of them well. The mere fact of involvement with a large circle of acquaintances is often thought to induce the sociological disease known as *anomie*.

An unexpected variant of this theory holds that the villager is thrown into close contact with most of his fellow villagers. This constitutes a large, *not* a small ambience, compared to the urbanite's limited circle of acquaintance. It would follow from the supposed inverse correlation of extensity and intensity that the villager's intimacy with his many compatriots is less than the city man's intimacy with his few selected friends. The villager is less dependent on the people he knows, and less likely to be demoralized if he loses their support or affection for any reason. Note that the villager wins either way.

The planner of residential neighborhoods must choose between alternative and inconsistent assumptions concerning the influence of neighborhood size on the intensity of neighboring. The question is usually resolved either by assuming an inverse relationship between extensity and intensity (the smaller the neighborhood the greater its intimacy) or by supposing that there is no relationship. Under the latter assumption, the larger the number of accessible neighbors, the more likely is a family to develop intimate relationships with some of them. The first assumption encourages the cul-de-sac pattern of suburban street design. The second inspires the multiple skyscraper type of low-rent public housing.

The data on neighborhood interaction in the twenty-five San Juan neighborhoods provide an opportunity for a test of several incompatible theories about the correlation of extensity and intensity.

These are:

1. *The Fund of Sociability Hypothesis* proposes an inverse correlation between extensity and intensity of interaction. An individual or family has a fixed fund of sociability (measured in units of disposable time and energy) available for interaction with others. This fund can be spread thin over a large number of casual acquaintances or concentrated on a small number of close friends. A finding that families with extensive neighboring relationships have low intensity scores—and vice versa—would support this hypothesis.

2. *The Rotarian Hypothesis* holds that popularity is cumu-

lative, and that—interactionally speaking—to him that hath shall be given. Subjects with large ambiences will be "sociometric stars" who attract choices from all sides and develop many intimate relationships. The isolates and deviates who know few of their neighbors are not likely to know any of them well.

3. *The Random Hypothesis.* If both of the foregoing hypotheses are plausible, they may balance each other out and the correlation between extensity and intensity of interaction may be insignificant. Alternatively, the factors which determine extensity may be quite different from those which determine intensity, so that knowing the size of a subject's ambience might tell us nothing about the intimacy of his relationships.

4. *Other Hypotheses:* It is also conceivable that the relationship between extensity and intensity might be curvilinear, or discontinuous, or dependent in some way on the absolute size of the ambience. For example, intensity might increase with ambience size in small groups, and decrease with ambience size in large groups.

Previous Studies

Although they remain unsettled, these questions are by no means new. Previous studies give us conflicting clues. Many years ago Lundberg[3] studied a village in Vermont and asked its inhabitants to name their "best friends." His subjects named an average of 2.3 best friends, with a range from 0 to 8. The choices were grouped in clusters of thirty to forty members, based on socio-economic characteristics. The results in these ambiences seemed to support the Fund of Sociability hypothesis.

"The conspicuous tendency . . . to make a few choices offers some support to the theory of limited social expansiveness. Aside from possible motives of expediency . . . it is also possible that the diffusion of one's social energies among a large group may weaken the intensity of one's emotional bonds with selected smaller groups." [4]

[3] George A. Lundberg and M. Steele, "Social Attraction Patterns in a Village," *Sociometry*, Vol. 1, January-April, 1938.
[4] *Ibid.*, p. 364.

The University Village studies, using the Neighborhood Interaction Scale, found no relationship at all between extensity and intensity of neighboring.[5]

Some indirect support for the Rotarian hypothesis can be found in a number of studies which show that individuals with high rates of neighborhood participation are likely to show higher than average participation in other kinds of voluntary association.

A careful study of the correlates of organization membership in rural neighborhoods by Christiansen concludes that:

"In individual tests of association between neighborhood membership and extent of participation in each of the twelve activities . . . eight items were found to be associated, church attendance, grocery purchases, participation in school-related organizations, participation in church related organizations, ball game attendance, family visiting and parties. Participation in dances, organizations other than church or school-related ones, mutual aid, and work exchange were not found to be characteristic of neighborhood members." [6]

Lionberger and Hassinger,[7] in a study of the diffusion of farm information, conclude that farms occupying focal positions in the neighborhood were most instrumental in the exchange of farm information. Such exchange was in turn related to high participation in local associations.

A study of neighborhood groups in relation to soil conservation activities by Mayo and Barnett [8] shows participation in one to be closely related to the other.

Additional evidence of correlation between neighboring and other forms of voluntary participation in rural neighborhoods, is reported by Kolb and Marshall,[9] Alexander and Nelson,[10] and Paul Landis.[11]

[5] Caplow and Forman, op. cit., Shimota, op. cit., Cole, op. cit.

[6] John R. Christiansen, "The Behavioral Correlates of Membership in Rural Neighborhoods," Rural Sociology, Vol. 22, March 1957.

[7] Hubert F. Lionberger and Edward Hassinger, "Neighborhoods as a Factor in the Diffusion of Farm Information in a Northeast Missouri Farming Community," Rural Sociology, Vol. 19, December 1954.

[8] S. C. Mayo and Wm. E. Barnett, "Neighborhood Groups: An Informal System of Communication," Rural Sociology, Vol. 17, 1952.

[9] J. H. Kolb and Douglas G. Marshall, Neighborhood-Community Relationships in Rural Society, Madison, Wisconsin, Agricultural Experiment Station Bulletin 154, 1944.

[10] Frank D. Alexander and Lowry Nelson, Rural Social Organization in Goodhue County, Minnesota, St. Paul, Agricultural Experiment Station Bulletin 401, 1949.

[11] Paul H. Landis, Rural Life in Process, New York, McGraw-Hill, 1940, pp. 167-82.

Similar findings emerge from urban studies. Bell and Boat, for example, compared informal social relationships, neighboring, and participation in formal organizations.[12] Although they did not study the association between extensity and intensity of interaction directly, their data suggest that high participation in one type of sociable activity is correlated with high participation in the others.[13] However, Form and Dansereau, in a study of union members, found some evidence that subjects most involved in union and plant activities are least involved in their neighborhoods.[14]

A review of neighboring studies by Dobriner leads him to the conclusion that:

"We have indicated that 'rural survivals,' heterogeneity, and the very size of the city set up conditions which may be conducive to neighboring. Many recent studies have already begun to show that neighboring is more common in cities than had been expected. It appears that the seeds of local intimacy have already been planted in much of the urban population.[15]

Findings of This Study

Table 1 (in the appendix to this chapter) shows intensity by total ambience size, for 484 families in the San Juan sample. The sixteen missing families were completely isolated; that is, they knew none of their neighbors by name and face. The table looks inscrutable at first glance but can be read easily enough as follows.

The figure in the first column, first row, tells us there are four families with an ambience size of one who have in-

[12] Wendell Bell and Marion B. Boat, "Urban Neighborhoods and Informal Social Relations," *American Journal of Sociology*, Vol. 62, January 1957.

[13] *ibid.*, see Tables 2 and 8.

[14] William H. Form and H. K. Dansereau, "Union Member Orientations and Patterns of Social Integration," *Industrial and Labor Relations Review*, Vol. 11, October 1957.

[15] William M. Dobriner (ed.), *The Suburban Community*, New York, Putnam's Sons, 1958, p. 128.

tensity scores of less than 2. (This may be a good place to recall that a score of 2 corresponds to regular conversation, 4 to common activities, and 6 to mutual visiting and entertaining.)

The figure in the last column, third row tells us there are twenty-one families with ambience sizes of eighteen or nineteen (maximum extensity) who have intensity scores between 3 and 4.

In each column of Table 1 the cell which includes the median case is circled. For ambiences including only a single neighbor, the median intensity is in the range of 5 to 6. For ambiences with two or three neighbors, the median intensity is in the range of 3 to 4, and so forth.

The Fund of Sociability hypothesis seems to gain support from these figures. *All* of the families with very high intensities (scale values of 5 or more) have small ambiences, consisting of five neighbors or less. Conversely, *all* of the families with very large ambiences (including sixteen or more neighbors) have rather low intensities (under 4).

On the other hand, the median intensity is strangely unaffected by increases of ambience size once we get beyond the tiny ambiences consisting of one, two or three neighbors. With one exception, the median intensity is the same for all of the larger ambience sizes.

If we were forced at this point to choose among the hypotheses, we would have to accept the Fund of Sociability hypothesis but in a very limited and qualified way, noting that the only subjects whose interaction with their neighbors is characterized by very high *average* intensity are those who associate with very few neighbors. For all others, the relationship between ambience size and intensity is not very striking. The families who interact with all of their neighbors (ambience sizes of eighteen or nineteen) show about the same median intensity as those who interact with a fourth, a third, or a half of their neighbors. This is really a rather remarkable finding when we consider that the larger ambiences might easily have been inflated by the inclusion of greeting acquaintances. In this instance, then, the lack of significant correlation is a curiosity which invites further examination.

Table 2 is a comparison of each family's total ambience with its active ambience (neighbors with whom a relationship is sustained at the level of 2 or higher). It is read in the following fashion. The first entry in the first column tells us that four of the families having an ambience size of one, did not have any active relationships. In the next column: of those families having a total ambience of two or three neighbors, eight had no active relationships, twelve had one active relationship and twenty-five had two or three. The number circled in each column shows where the median case (arrayed by the size of active ambience) falls. Looking across the table, we note a curious phenomenon. The absolute number of active relationships increase more or less regularly with increasing ambience size, but *not* proportionately. For example, the median family with a total ambience of ten neighbors has more active as well as more casual relationships than the median family with an ambience of five neighbors. However, while the total ambience is twice as large, the active ambience is only half again as large. This pattern is consistent across the table.

What we seem to see here are diminishing returns for sociability. A family which widens its circle of *acquaintances* may hope to increase the number of its friends, but the increment of friendship, so to speak, is less than proportionate to each added increment of acquaintanceship.

This provides an interesting commentary on the hypothesis we want to test. Table 1 shows that the average intensity of neighboring relationships declines as the number of relationships increases. Table 2 makes it clear that this decline is accomplished by a decreasing *proportion* of relationships with higher scores, not by a decrease in the number of intimate relationships.

This state of affairs seems to require a compromise between the Fund of Sociability and the Rotarian hypotheses. As the number of relationships increases, their average intensity decreases and this must be explained, in one sense or another, by the limited resources available to meet the time and energy costs of sociability. However, it is equally apparent that people with larger ambiences are doubly blessed (insofar as interaction is a blessing) since on the average they will enjoy a greater number of both intimate and casual relationships.

This view gains further support from Table 3 wherein each family's total ambience is compared with its intimate ambience (neighbors with whom a relationship is sustained at the level of 4 or higher). It is read in the same way as the previous table. We discover, for example, that of the forty-five families interacting with only two or three neighbors, twenty-six had no confirmed intimate relationships, fifteen had one such relationship and four families had two or three such relationships.[16]

The pattern is the same, only somewhat distorted by arithmetical limitations. It is certainly possible that as ambience sizes increased above twenty, the number of intimate relationships would remain constant or decline, but we have no way of determining this here. All that can be said with assurance is that in these small neighborhoods, intimate relationships show a tendency to increase with increasing size of the total ambience but much more slowly than the active relationships described in Table 2. Not only the trend of the medians, but the shape of the distribution shows a positive although imperfect correlation between the total number of relationships and the number of intimate relatonships. The correlation may seem redundant. It is not so at all, since under the Fund of Sociability hypothesis, we would expect a negative correlation and under the Random hypothesis, no correlation.

[16] The reader may wonder why awkward double captions like 2-3 have been adopted for these tables. The only motive was to reduce them to convenient size. The interpretation is precisely the same if we substitute the 19 x 19 cell version of the tables.

APPENDIX

Intensity and Extensity of Neighboring

TABLE 1

Intensity of Neighboring by Total Ambience Size*
in a Sample of San Juan Neighborhoods (N = 484 Families)

Mean Confirmed Scores	*Total Ambience Size*									
	1	2-3	4-5	6-7	8-9	10-11	12-13	14-15	16-17	18-19
1.00-1.99	4	14	18	8	7	12	13	13	53	43
2.00-2.99	3	7	14	11	13	24	11	9	13	39
3.00-3.99	3	17	9	10	6	6	8	13	11	21
4.00-4.99		4	8	4	2	6	3	1		
5.00-5.99	4	1	2							
6.00	10	2	4							
TOTAL	24	45	55	33	28	48	35	36	77	103

* Chi-square, computed on a 3 x 3 table (ambience size: 1-7, 8-15, 16-19; Intensity score: 1.99-under, 2.00-2.99, 3.00-over) = 51.03, df = 4, p < .001 $\gamma = -.37$

TABLE 2

Relationship Between Total Ambience Size and Active Ambience Size

Active Ambience Size	Total Ambience Size									
	1	2-3	4-5	6-7	8-9	10-11	12-13	14-15	16-17	18-19
0	4	8	10		1		1	2	5	7
1	20	12	8	2		2			17	3
2-3		25	20	10	9	5	3	3	10	4
4-5			17	16	3	15	9	9	1	15
6-7				5	10	17	10	3	7	4
8-9					5	8	6	6	2	3
10-11						1	5	5	15	6
12-13							1	7	8	6
14-15								1	11	5
16-17									1	22
18-19										28
TOTAL	24	45	55	33	28	48	35	36	77	103

TABLE 3

Relationship Between Total Ambience Size and Intimate Ambience Size

Intimate Ambience Size	Total Ambience Size									
	1	2-3	4-5	6-7	8-9	10-11	12-13	14-15	16-17	18-19
0	10	28	22	9	6	9	9	7	20	24
1	14	13	14	12	11	13	3	8	25	14
2-3		4	16	8	9	15	11	5	19	30
4-5			3	4	1	6	7	6	2	14
6-7					1	4	3	8		8
8-9						1	2	1	8	2
10-11								1	3	3
12-13										7
14-15										1
16-17										
18-19										
TOTAL	24	45	55	33	28	48	35	36	77	103

6 Reciprocal Choice

The Choosers and the Chosen

This chapter concerns the pattern of discrepancies between pairs of neighbors reporting their mutual relationship. Once again, the basic data consist of interview responses obtained from 500 families located in twenty-five neighborhoods in the San Juan Metropolitan Area. A respondent in each family described their relationships with nineteen families living in contiguous households, and on the basis of these descriptions, the interviewer assigned each relationship a score on the Neighborhood Interaction Scale. Thus, for any pair of families in the same neighborhood we have a pair of reports about their mutual relationship, and two independently derived scores.

If there were no errors either in the respondent's descriptions of their own behavior, or their perception of the be-

havior of others, or the interviewer's ability to understand
and classify what he heard, there would be *no* discrepancies.
The descriptions of a relationship by either participant
would be identical and both responses would be given the
same score. As a matter of fact, in slightly more than half of
the reported relationships, the descriptions of the two participants *were* given the same score, and almost half of the remainder differ by only a single scale interval. Without substantial agreement, the data would hardly be worth analyz-
ing.

That the subjects often agree in reporting their relationship does not diminish the interest of those cases in which
they fail to agree. The statistical (and even the non-statisti-
cal) analyst expects to find an orderly pattern in any set of
systematic errors. The discrepancies between neighbors' reports of their mutual relationship certainly constitute a set
of systematic errors and invite us to explain their distribution.

We want to know, among other things, whether there are
any predictable differences between families that report
closer relationships with their neighbors than their neighbors
report with them, and families that report lesser relationships
with their neighbors than their neighbors report with them?

We also want to know whether there are predictable differences between the family whose informant gives a "high"
report and the family whose informant gives "low" report
concerning the same relationship.

There are good reasons for expecting differences of this
kind. A number of sociometric studies have shown high
status persons to be over-chosen, and low status persons to
be under-chosen in preferential choices. While the Neighborhood Interaction Scale is supposed to report actual interaction
rather than interaction preferences, it is clear that discrepancies in the reports of the two parties may reflect preference,
avoidance, or wish fulfillment.

It is also reasonable to suppose that neighboring relationships have greater functional significance for some families
than for others and that consequently, the pressures leading
to discrepant reports will vary from one situation to another.

Buried in this last assertion is an assumption about the relationship between "real" neighboring behavior and reported neighboring behavior. For simplicity's sake, we will
assume that the actual behavior in a given relationship lies
somewhere between the limits set by the discrepant reports
of the two participants. Of course, there are other possibilities. It may be (a) that both parties understate the relation-

ship, in the sense that the "real" relationship is at a higher level than either report; or (b) both parties overstate their relationship, the "real" relationship being lower than either report or (c) the "real" relationship is at the level of the higher report; or (d) the "real" relationship is at the level of the lower report.

Given our assumption—that the "real" relationship is at some indeterminate point between the pair of reports—it is reasonable to speak of the higher as an overstatement, the lower as an understatement.

Pattern of Discrepancy

Table 1 (in the appendix to this chapter) shows the distribution of discrepant reports. As noted above, the subjects are moderately consistent in reporting mutual relationships. Only twenty-six percent of the total relationships showed discrepancies of two or more scale intervals between the report of the participants.

A considerable proportion of all the recorded discrepancies refer to relationships scored 1 on one side and zero on the other. Examination of the Neighborhood Interaction Scale shows that this difference (but no other) can occur without any error of observation. In other words, it is quite possible for A to know B by name and face while B cannot identify A. Table 2 overcomes this difficulty by omitting all cases with paired scores 1-0. Using this standard, the proportion of relationships identically described by participants rises to fifty-seven percent.

The first question is whether some respondents have a general tendency to overstate or understate their neighboring relationships. This question can be answered by computing each family's mean discrepancy, by taking the total of neighboring scores "given" by Family X to other families, subtracting the total of neighboring scores "received" by Family X from other families, and dividing by the number of relationships involved. The figure obtained represents the tendency of the respondent in Family X to overstate or understate relationships. The distribution of mean discrepancies, from inspection, is conspicuously normal. The mean of the distribution is 0.01; the standard deviation is 1.09. Both the median and the mode are 0.00. There are 237 cases deviating positively from zero; 233 cases deviating negatively.[1] Families with positive mean discrepancies can be described as overchosen. Their neighbors claim closer relationships with them than they are willing to admit. Families with negative mean discrepancies are underchosen. They claim closer relationships with their neighbors than their neighbors are willing to concede.

Who Are the Chosen?

The naive expectation is that families of high prestige[2] relative to their neighbors will be overchosen and families of low prestige will be underchosen. A family's prestige, being partly determined by that of its intimates, might be protected by consistently overstating relationships with social superiors and minimizing relationships with inferiors.[3]

Table 3 tests this expectation. It compares mean discrepancies, divided into high, middle and low categories, with the occupational level of family heads (roughly divided into white collar and manual). The results are completely unexpected. The white collar families are more often overchosen, but they are also more often *underchosen*. In other words, a high prestige family is likely to be either overchosen or underchosen while a low prestige family is more likely to *agree* with its neighbors about the description of its relationships.

This curious result is not a statistical quirk. About a dozen different prestige indicators were cross-tabulated against dis-

[1] The handful of isolated families in the sample who neither knew or were known by any of their neighbors are omitted from the analysis.
[2] A full description of social stratification in San Juan is available in Melvin M. Tumin and Arnold Feldman, *Social Class and Social Change in Puerto Rico*, Princeton, Princeton University Press, 1961.
[3] Presumably these tendencies go beyond reporting to interaction and it is easy to visualize the lower ranking member of an unequal pair seeking to increase the intimacy of a relationship while the higher ranking member seeks to reduce it. See, for example, the classic episode of the two dinner parties in Sinclair Lewis' *Babbitt*.

crepancies computed in various ways, and broken down at varying intervals. The results remain the same, no matter how the data are re-arranged.

Our tentative explanation is that prestige differences may either hinder or facilitate neighboring, depending on the interactive structure of the neighborhood. In a well-integrated and homogeneous neighborhood,[4] high-prestige families may be acknowledged as models, and overchosen. In another situation, the possession of socially valued characteristics may exclude a family from the circle of its slightly envious or suspicious neighbors, so that the high-prestige family will be consistently underchosen.

Skin color[5] is one major social characteristic which follows a different pattern. As Table 4 shows, white families are consistently overchosen in relation to non-white families. Since there are no neighborhoods with a majority of non-whites, this tabulation reflects the interaction between whites and non-whites and suggests a tendency to segregation by color, which is independent of prestige factors.

In the one case where the cause of discrepancies ought to be self-evident, it turns out to be so. When we tabulate the mean discrepancy against moving intentions, as in Table 5, we discover that families intending to move consistently underchoose their neighbors, while families who intend to stay consistently overchoose their potentially more mobile neighbors. This is a kind of "anticipatory mobility." Families intending to leave the neighborhood have begun to disentangle themselves from its interaction network.

As we might by now expect, overchosen and underchosen families tend to be found in the same neighborhoods.

Taking overchosen and underchosen families together, there are eleven neighborhoods having seven or more of these families and eleven other neighborhoods having five or less. The neighborhoods with a high proportion of overchosen and underchosen families show an average ambience size of 8.0 while those with a low proportion have an average ambience size of 12.3. The difference is highly significant. Table 6 shows the relationship between ambience size and mean discrepancy when families in the sample are analyzed one by one. Again we find an association between discrepancies and extensity of neighboring. Underchosen and overchosen families have much smaller ambiences on the average.

Discrepant reports about neighboring appear to arise

[4] As in many of the studies cited above.
[5] As classified by the interviewer.

partly from social preference and avoidances, and partly from ignorance. The smaller the average ambience, and the greater the variations of prestige and other differentiating characteristics, the fewer families will be able to develop an accurate idea of their own place in the network of relationships. This interpretation, of course, is highly tentative, although the tendency to discrepant reports in small ambiences is unmistakable.

If we consider relationships rather than families, we again discover several types of regularity. The sample—considered in this way—contains a grand total of 4750 neighboring relationships, 1820 of them between families conspicuously unequal in educational achievement.[6] Sixty-five percent of these unequal relationships were discrepantly reported, compared to forty percent of equal relationships. The difference is significant. The higher ranking member of the unequal pair was overchosen in 662 cases, and underchosen in 529 cases. This difference is significant, and in the expected direction, although not very impressive.

Another analysis involved intimate relationships (having a value of 4 or more on the Neighborhood Interaction Scale) with or without educational equality.

The results are shown on Table 7. There is a significant tendency for families to select interaction partners at the same educational level but the table shows that this is only an inclination—not a rule. Analysis by housing quality shows the same pattern. Slightly more than half of all the relationships reported involved educational inequality, although the distribution of the criterion is such that every family in the sample might have confined its intimate relationships to other families of equal educational achievement without much effect on the total volume of interaction.

We can only surmise how the equivalent data from communities elsewhere in the world would look. It seems likely that when such data are available, they will often show a much higher degree of segregation by social class than appears in San Juan, where stratification exerts a pervasive but minor influence on the pattern of neighborhood interaction.

---

[6] Families were classified on the basis of average educational achievement of husband and wife into three categories: 0-8 years, 9-12 years, 13-over years. Two families within any of these categories were considered to be equal. Two families which crossed any two of these categories were considered to be unequal. For a very full discussion of the educational criterion for stratification in San Juan, see Melvin M. Tumin and Arnold Feldman, *op. cit.*

APPENDIX

Distribution of Discrepancies in Reports of Neighboring Relationships

TABLE 1

Number and Proportion of Discrepant Reports
by Size of Discrepancy

Size of Discrepancy	N	%
0	2448	51.54
1	1087	22.88
2	577	12.15
3	353	7.43
4	143	3.01
5	77	1.62
6	65	1.37
TOTAL	4750	100.00

TABLE 2

Number and Proportion of Discrepant Reports
by Size of Discrepancy (0-1 Reports Omitted)

Size of Discrepancy	N	%
0	2448	57.24
1	614	14.36
2	577	13.49
3	353	8.25
4	143	3.34
5	77	1.80
6	65	1.52
TOTAL	4277	100.00

TABLE 3

Discrepancy Scores by Occupation of Head of Household

		Discrepancy Score		
		Overchosen	"Balanced"	Underchosen
Occupation*	High	113	79	105
	Low	54	83	55

$X^2 = 14.72$, df $= 2$, p $< .01$

* "Retired" omitted.

TABLE 4

Discrepancy Scores by Wife's Color

		Discrepancy Score		
		Overchosen	"Balanced"	Underchosen
Wife's Color	White	145	120	126
	Non-white	23	44	36

$X^2 = 8.96$, df $= 2$, p $< .02$

TABLE 5

Discrepancy Scores by Moving Intention

		Discrepancy Score		
		Overchosen	"Balanced"	Underchosen
Moving Intention	Move	75	72	47
	Stay	91	93	116

$X^2 = 11.16$, df $= 2$, p $< .01$
$\gamma = .23$

TABLE 6

Discrepancy Scores by Total Ambience Size

		Discrepancy Score		
		Overchosen	"Balanced"	Underchosen
Total Ambience Size	0-5	59	35	42
	6-over	109	130	121

$X^2 = 8.42$, df $= 2$, p $< .02$

TABLE 7

Intimate Relationships Among Families of Equal
and Unequal Education

		Intimate Relationships	
		Actual	Expected*
Education	Equal	280	241.7
	Unequal	214	252.3

$X^2 = 11.88$, df $= 1$, p $< .001$

* Based on possible relationships.

7 Residential Satisfaction

Residential Satisfaction

Most of our information about residential satisfaction is based on two questions in the interview: "Do you consider this neighborhood a good place to live? Why or why not?" and "Do you intend to stay here permanently?"

Satisfaction and Moving Intentions

The distribution of responses to the question "is your neighborhood a good place to live" is heavily skewed in the direction of satisfaction.

The responses to the two questions are highly correlated. [Table 1] Most of those who intend to move are dissatisfied.[1] Most of those who intend to stay are satisfied. However, there are clear-cut contrary cases. In the older neighborhoods and the slums, there are many trapped families, profoundly dissatisfied but unable to move because of home ownership or age or insufficient resources. Some cases combine all of these elements. The sample includes an elderly couple in La Zona. Their house would probably not attract any buyer. If it did, it would not bring enough for the purchase of a house elsewhere. It can not be exchanged for a rented unit because the husband is retired and his pension barely covers food and clothing.

Another typical situation in which moving intentions are not explained by dissatisfaction with the neighborhood is that of the upwardly mobile family just at the point of passing into a higher social stratum. They are likely to have high neighboring scores and considerable attachment to their present neighborhood, but have begun to detach themselves in preparation for the long step into a different milieu.

In a previous chapter we saw that families intending to move tend to "underchoose" their neighbors. The tables show that moving intentions and extensity of neighboring are inversely related so that those who intend to move have smaller ambiences on the average than those who intend to stay. This represents, on the one hand, the abandonment of neighborhood affiliations by families on their way out; on the other hand, the tendency for families with fewer neighboring relationships to be less firmly rooted. The relationship holds whether we consider intimate neighbors or all neighbors. [Tables 2 and 3] When we compare moving intentions to the size of the intimate ambience, the degree of association is unchanged. As we have previously observed there is a significant positive relationship between intensity of neighboring and neighborhood evaluation.[2] *People who have close relationships with their neighbors are more satisfied with their neighborhoods as places to live.*

---

[1] The abundant evidence that intra-city moves are usually due to dissatisfaction, or in other words, that most residential mobility can be explained in terms of *push* rather than *pull*, is summarized in Nelson N. Foote, et. al., *Housing Choices and Housing Constraints*, New York, McGraw Hill, 1960, especially chapter 6, "The Consumer Votes by Moving."

[2] See Tables 17 and 18, Appendix to Chapter Four.

The Time Factor

Families who have lived more than five years at their present addresses express much less intention to move than those who have lived in one place for a shorter time, as is shown in Table 4. This finding appears at first to be a statistical artifact, on the supposition that living in the same house for a long time shows a retroactive lack of intention to move. On closer view, it turns out to be meaningful. It is entirely conceivable that if neighborhood dissatisfaction were the rule, the patience of the average family might be gradually eroded in such a way as to produce a steady increase of moving intentions with increasing tenure. As an analogy, we would expect to find an almost perfect correlation between the "tenure" of apples on a tree and their "intention" to fall.

Neighborhood evaluation also rises with increasing tenure although more slowly and not significantly. This association is more impressive than it seems because the quality of buildings in San Juan is inversely correlated with age—partly because of the rapid deterioration of light construction in the tropics, and partly because housing standards have been rising steadily in Puerto Rico.

Moving intentions are also strongly influenced by the length of time the husband and wife—considered separately or together—have lived in San Juan. [Tables 5 and 6] An overwhelming majority of San Juan adults were born elsewhere in the Island and migrated to the city. Various studies suggest that the migrant's adjustment to his urban environment tends to improve over a long period of time.[3] His adjustment to a particular neighborhood is a part—and an essential part—of this larger process.

There is also some relationship between the wife's—but not the husband's—total duration of urban residence and neighborhood evaluation. [Table 7] The evaluation, after all, was made by the wife, and certainly misrepresented the husband's attitude in some cases.

[3] See especially Tumin, op. cit.

The Correlates of Satisfaction

The absolute distribution of residential satisfaction as it appears in these tables has not been sufficiently stressed. Most of these San Juan families, many of whom live in neighborhoods considered "squalid" and "shocking" by outside observers, express a degree of satisfaction with their surroundings which borders on complacency. The percentage distribution of responses to the question, "Is this neighborhood a good place to live?" was as follows:

Classification of Responses	Percent of Sample
Affirmative	69
Qualified	18
Negative	13
TOTAL	100

The distribution of moving intentions is somewhat more complex. The expressed intention to stay in the present neighborhood or to move was characterized as definite—involving elements of planning or commitment—or indefinite —involving only a preference. A large proportion of intentions to move are indefinite. Intentions to stay are usually definite. The distribution is as follows:

	Percent of Sample		
	Definite	Indefinite	Total
Intend to move	23	16	39
Intend to stay	58	3	61
TOTAL	81	19	100

HOUSEHOLD COMPOSITION: There is a significant association between neighborhood dissatisfaction or intention to move, and the number of children under eighteen in the household. [Tables 8 and 9] In other words, the more young children in a family, the more likely are the parents to be dissatisfied with the neighborhood and to intend to move.[4]

Families with small children have changing needs and re-

[4] Fertility being high in this urban population, there are very few young childless couples to be found in this sample. Only twelve of eighty-three wives under age thirty have no children.

quirements. As these develop, they are likely to discover unsuitable features in the neighborhood which would not be of
serious concern to a household of adults. The interviews
contain frequent comments that: "The street with all those
trucks is not safe for children to play on" or "with that bar
on the corner, this is no place to bring up an adolescent female."

These findings are exactly parallel to those of North American studies and Rossi's comment on his Philadelphia findings
is entirely applicable here.

"The housing needs of a *young* household are most likely to be
'out of balance,' as it were, with its actual housing. This is a
period in a family life cycle where the greatest amount of change
in household size and composition takes place. It is also the
period in which the household, because of the financial demands
made upon it by these rapid changes in size and composition, is
least likely to bring housing into line with its needs." [5]

Total household size also shows consistent and significant
correlation with neighborhood evaluation and moving intentions. The larger families are *less* satisfied and *more*
likely to move. [Tables 10 and 11] The *very* large families
(seven persons or more) who comprise slightly over a tenth
of the sample, show about the same incidence of moving
intentions as the very small families, although their average
level of satisfaction is much lower. The common sense explanation is that they can not readily find new accomoda-
tions of suitable size.

As Tables 12 and 13 show, incomplete families, either
wives without husbands, or parents without children, show
greater satisfaction with their neighborhoods and less interest in moving. On the average, these families are older,
smaller, and less able to find new accommodations. The relationships of wife's age, and husband's age, to satisfaction
and moving intention are shown in Tables 14-16.

SOCIAL CLASS: The most useful indicators of class position in modern Puerto Rico are educational level (of both
husband and wife), occupation (of the principal breadwinner), and income (total and per capita). They are closely
related to each other and to both extensity and intensity of
neighboring. They are also related to residential evaluation
and moving intentions, but rather intricately.

If we dichotomize the population into those with and

[5] Peter H. Rossi, *Why Families Move: A Study in the Social Psychology
of Urban Residential Mobility*, Glencoe, The Free Press, 1955, p. 72.

without education past high school, as in Table 17, the more educated show significantly higher neighborhood satisfaction. The same tendency exists, but non-significantly, with respect to moving intentions. However, if we trichotomize educational achievement so as to focus on the group of families with intermediate education (husband and wife average between six and twelve years of schooling) as in Table 18, this middle category shows a higher proportion intending to move, compared with those above or below.

Similar results are obtained when residential satisfaction is tabulated by the occupation of the principal breadwinner. High occupational status is associated with favorable neighborhood evaluation, and with the intention of remaining in the neighborhood. [Table 19] Families intending to move are again disproportionately concentrated in the middle occupational levels. [Table 20]

Income data, both total and per capita, present much the same pattern. [Tables 21-24]

Rossi's comments on Philadelphia are again literally applicable to the San Juan data.

"Families moving up the 'occupational ladder' are particularly sensitive to the social aspects of location and use residential mobility to bring their residences into line with their prestige needs. In the findings of this study, some of the households were strongly dissatisfied with their housing and social environment, and were expressing the way in which their home no longer fitted in with their social aspirations." [6]

RELIGIOSITY: As Table 25 shows, there is a clear association between residential satisfaction and religious affiliation. Catholics (who constitute the overwhelming majority of the sample) express consistently more satisfaction with their neighborhoods than Protestants. However, there is no significant difference between Catholics and Protestants in their inclination to move. Protestants are very much in a minority and not segregated. Presumably, they have no more inclination to move than their Catholic neighbors because their minority position would not ordinarily be remedied by a change of neighborhood.[7]

Church *attendance*, as distinguished from affiliation is associated positively with neighborhood satisfaction and in-

[6] *Ibid.*, p. 179.
[7] Comparable findings were reported for a sample of neighborhoods in Israel by Judith Shuval in a paper presented at the 1961 meetings of the American Sociological Association.

versely with moving intentions, either because frequent and regular church attendance confers prestige, or because it indicates adjustment to the social environment. [Tables 26 and 27]

HOUSING: As we consider the influence of the quality of housing on residential satisfaction, it becomes increasingly clear that satisfaction with the neighborhood is determined by the physical and social characteristics of the neighborhood, not of the family's own home. On the other hand, the intention to move may be due to the disadvantages of the neighborhood, or of the dwelling unit, or of both. Thus, we can expect a closer association between the quality of housing and moving intentions than between the quality of housing and neighborhood satisfaction, and this is precisely what we find. The quality of housing is closely (and inversely) related to moving intentions, as well as to neighborhood evaluation. [Tables 28 and 29]

The influence of dwelling type (single or multiple) on neighborhood satisfaction and moving intentions follows a similar pattern. [Tables 30 and 31] Families in single dwellings have less interest in moving than families in multiple units. They also show somewhat higher neighborhood satisfaction but this difference is less well-marked, and may be due to clustering. The occupants of public low-rent housing projects show even less intention to move than the occupants of private single-family homes and much higher neighborhood satisfaction. Separating out the residents of public projects has the effect of sharpening the differences in residential satisfaction between families in private, single and multiple dwelling units.[8]

It might be supposed that the differences between families occupying single and multiple dwellings might derive from the satisfactions inherent in home ownership. Forty-five percent of the families in the sample own their own homes and most of these are single family dwellings. There is no significant association between home ownership and residential satisfaction. However, as common sense requires, there *is* a significant relationship between home ownership and intention to stay in place. [Table 32]

Another measure of the quality of dwelling units is bed-

[8] This is contrary to much of the experience with public "project" housing in the United States—often characterized by acute neighborhood dissatisfaction. For a closer view of tenant adjustment to low-rent public housing in San Juan, see Kurt W. Back, *Slums Projects and People*, Durham, North Carolina, Duke University Press, 1962.

room density, the ratio of persons to sleeping rooms in the family dwelling, and a direct measure of overcrowding. The relationship between bedroom density and moving intentions is spectacular. [Table 33] The proportion of families intending to move rises from thirty-one percent among families with bedroom densities of 1.5 or less to sixty-one percent among families with bedroom densities of 3.0 or more. The relationship between bedroom density and neighborhood satisfaction is such that the higher the density, the lower the satisfaction. [Table 34]

IMPROVEMENTS: The Improvement Index[9] is a composite estimate of "the convenience of life" in a neighborhood, based on the presence or absence of public services (paving, sewers, lighting, sidewalks, transportation, shopping facilities) and of nuisances (noise, odors, heavy traffic, dirt). When we compare this index with neighborhood satisfaction, the results are strikingly clear. The higher the level of neighborhood improvements, the more neighborhood satisfaction is recorded. [Table 35] Moving intentions follow exactly the same pattern—the more amenities and the fewer nuisances the lower the proportion of residents wanting to move. [Table 36]

Some, but not all the components of this scale can be separately tabulated. The correlations of neighborhood satisfaction with availability of transportation, length of the journey to work, convenience of the journey to work, and convenience of transportation to school,[10] are all moderately significant. The *length* of the journey to work and the journey to school are also significantly correlated with moving intentions but not the *convenience* of the journey to work or the journey to school. It appears that the subjective fact of convenience as distinct from the objective fact of distance from work or school is not important enough to influence a family's moving intentions, although it may play a part in the choice of a new location.

HOMOGENEITY AND HETEROGENEITY: This study was designed with the assumption that homogeneity would be crucial in explaining neighborhood structure. On the basis of previous studies, we expected that homogeneous neighborhoods would show more neighboring than heterogeneous neighborhoods and that intimate neighboring relationships would ordinarily involve families with similar social characteristics. Neither of these expectations is fully supported by

9 Described in Chapter Four.
10 For the eldest child in families having children at school.

the data, although families living in homogeneous neighborhoods show slightly more intensity in their neighboring.
Conceivably San Juaneros may be less class-conscious in their
choice of friends and neighbors than the inhabitants of cities
elsewhere. The non-nucleated metropolitan structure suggests this possibility. Conceivably also, our sample is a
sample of heterogeneous neighborhoods, either by chance or
because of the larger non-nucleated pattern. Certainly, it
does not compare with certain United States suburbs populated by a uniform stratum of closed families having male
heads between twenty-five and thirty-five who are the sole
breadwinners, and in white collar occupations, all husbands and some wives having college degrees and all families having not less than one nor more than three children
under the age of ten. So far as we know, this degree of
homogeneity is never even approached in San Juan.

In view of the findings, it is interesting to note that
homogeneity is perceived by the respondents as a favorable
neighborhood characteristic. This is suggested by dozens of
responses to the open-ended question on neighborhood
satisfaction and confirmed by a significant relationship between neighborhood homogeneity and neighborhood satisfaction, and a moderately significant relationship between
heterogeneity and moving intentions. [Tables 37 and 38]

Local Peculiarities

The proportion of respondents expressing unqualified satisfaction with their neighborhood runs from five percent in
La Zona to one hundred percent in Sagrado Corazón. The
former is extraordinarily distant from any paved street or
means of public transportation, with an absolute minimum
of public facilities and a variety of public nuisances. There
is little neighboring, and considerable friction between the
disorderly and orderly elements of the population. Sagrado
Corazón is a middle-income neighborhood with excellent
facilities of every kind, conveniently located near the business center of Santurce. It is bounded by a luxurious district on one side and a belt of deteriorated housing on the

other. The interaction network is dominated by two separate cliques.

Intention to move was unanimous in Pozo del Hato since at the time the interviews were made, it was slated for early demolition to make room for a highway. The inhabitants were resigned to relocation although some of them took a rather odd view of the matter:

"It used to be a good place to live but not any more. Now it is a slum because they are clearing it."

Disregarding this special case, the highest proportion of families intending to move is in Mercado, a slum area in Old San Juan. It has a well-developed network of interaction and little internal conflict, but is close to a transient area which the residents identify with vice and disorder. Several of the respondents are prostitutes.

The lowest proportion of families intending to move was found in Monacillo Urbano, a brand new sub-division near the periphery of the metropolitan area. Its population is young, prosperous, well-educated, and consists of small families in single family houses. It has a dense and continuous interaction network. The residents regard themselves individually and collectively as socially privileged.

Summary and Conclusions

The rank order correlation of residential satisfaction and inclinations to move *taken by neighborhoods* (rho based on rank ordering of percentages) is — .49, a moderate degree of association under the circumstances. It is evident from thematic and statistical evidence that neighborhood satisfaction is a function of the objective characteristics of the neighborhood—physical, locational and social—while intention to move is determined both by the characteristics of the neighborhood and the problems and needs of the individual family.

A number of general observations may be relevant.

1. Not a single respondent in the entire sample objects to *too much* neighborhood interaction. Even in those neighborhoods with the most highly developed networks of in-

teraction, neighboring is still perceived as voluntary and conceived in terms of mutual helpfulness rather than social control. On the other hand, in neighborhoods with low interaction, there are many favorable comments on the theme that "people here don't bother you." Whether this is a compensatory reaction or reflects a real desire for privacy is a question beyond the scope of the data.

2. The attitudes reported with regard to residential satisfaction seem to us to be predominantly rational. All of the neighborhood characteristics which turn out to be related to satisfaction and dissatisfaction are functionally relevant. They do not indicate excessive preoccupation with status-seeking, or any perceptual distortion of reality.

3. The physical isolation of a neighborhood appears to be viewed in two ways—favorably insofar as it excludes outsiders and unfavorably insofar as it bars access to outside facilities. Seen in this perspective, the major problem of neighborhood planning is how to isolate the residential neighborhood from irrelevant traffic while preserving easy access to other parts of the city.

4. The amenity of life in a residential area can not be judged by casual, outside observation. The present sample includes slums whose inhabitants are extremely satisfied with their surroundings and middle income districts with prevailing dissatisfaction. Although neighborhood satisfaction tends to be higher in more prosperous neighborhoods, the incidence of satisfaction or dissatisfaction in a particular neighborhood can not be predicted without taking into account the particular requirements of a particular population.

The results presented in this chapter present indirect support for the theory presented by the Useems and Gibson[11] that:

"Residential mobility . . . is not then *per se* a stressful process leading to anomie, as it has sometimes been claimed, but actually a resource for occupationally upwardly mobile men; for moving enables them to activate the supporting neighborhood functions appropriate for their changing occupational role."

The *middle* groups on income, occupation, and educa-

[11] Ruth Hill Useem, John Useem, and Duane L. Gibson, "The Function of Neighboring for the Middle-Class Male," *Human Organization*. Vol. 19, Summer 1960. For more specific evidence regarding San Juan, see Division de Educación de la Communidad. *San Juan: La Cuidad que Rebasa sus Murallas,* 1957.

tion show consistently greater interest in moving than either their more fortunate or less fortunate neighbors. On the other hand, they demonstrate considerable satisfaction with the neighborhoods they intend to leave.

The notion of residential mobility as an adjustive process is strongly buttressed another way by our finding that residential satisfaction, however measured, increases with both age and length of residence. Once again the optimism that runs like a bright thread through the fabric of Puerto Rican society is statistically justified. With the passage of time, the San Juan family becomes increasingly satisfied with the particular place in the city to which its wanderings have led.

APPENDIX

Correlates of Residential Satisfaction

TABLE 1

Satisfaction with Neighborhood by Moving Intention

		Satisfaction		
		Low	Medium	High
Moving Intention	Move	50	41	104
	Stay	13	49	239

$$X^2 = 55.45, df = 2, p < .001$$
$$\gamma = .55$$

TABLE 2

Moving Intention by Size of Ambience

		Moving Intention	
		Move	Stay
Size of Ambience	0-11	108	139
	12-over	88	163

$$X^2 = 3.91, df = 1, p < .05$$
$$\gamma = .18$$

TABLE 3

Moving Intention by Size of Intimate Ambience

		Moving Intention	
		Move	Stay
Size of Intimate Ambience	0	76	82
	1	49	79
	2-over	71	141

$$X^2 = 8.18, df = 2, p < .05$$
$$\gamma = .21$$

TABLE 4

Moving Intention by Household Tenure

		Moving Intention	
		Move	Stay
Household Tenure	0-60 months	126	110
	61 months-over	70	191

$X^2 = 36.63$, df $= 1$, p $< .001$
$\gamma = .52$

TABLE 5

Moving Intention by Husband's San Juan Tenure

		Moving Intention	
		Move	Stay
Husband's San Juan Tenure	10 years less	32	30
	11-20 years	41	40
	21 years-over	81	134

$X^2 = 6.28$, df $= 2$, p $< .05$
$\gamma = .23$

TABLE 6

Moving Intention by Wife's San Juan Tenure

		Moving Intention	
		Move	Stay
Wife's San Juan Tenure	10 years-less	51	42
	11-20 years	43	57
	21 years-over	101	200

$X^2 = 14.12$, df $= 2$, p $< .001$
$\gamma = .30$

TABLE 7

Satisfaction with Neighborhood by Wife's San Juan Tenure

		Satisfaction		
		Low	Medium	High
Wife's San Juan Tenure	10 years-less	19	19	55
	11-20 years	15	23	62
	21 years-over	28	48	223

$X^2 = 13.09$, df $= 4$, p $< .02$
$\gamma = .26$

TABLE 8

Satisfaction with Neighborhood by Number of Children Under 18

| | | Satisfaction | | |
		Low	Medium	High
Number of Children Under 18	0-1	28	39	209
	2-over	35	51	133

$$X^2 = 12.87, df = 2, p < .01$$
$$\gamma = .30$$

TABLE 9

Moving Intention by Number of Children Under 18

| | | Moving Intention | |
		Move	Stay
Number of Children Under 18	0-1	87	190
	2-over	109	111

$$X^2 = 16.88, df = 1, p < .001$$
$$\gamma = -.36$$

TABLE 10

Satisfaction with Neighborhood by Household Size

| | | Satisfaction | | |
		Low	Medium	High
Household Size	1-4	30	50	219
	5-over	33	40	124

$$X^2 = 6.88, df = 2, p < .05$$
$$\gamma = -.23$$

TABLE 11

Moving Intention by Household Size

		Moving Intention	
		Move	Stay
Household Size	1-4	103	197
	5-over	93	105

$X^2 = 7.97$, df $= 1$, p $< .01$
$\gamma = -.26$

TABLE 12

Satisfaction with Neighborhood by Family Composition

		Satisfaction		
		Low	Medium	High
Family Composition	Incomplete	17	28	149
	Complete	46	62	194

$X^2 = 9.01$, df $= 2$, p $< .02$
$\gamma = -.28$

TABLE 13

Moving Intention by Family Composition

		Moving Intention	
		Move	Stay
Family Composition	Incomplete	58	137
	Complete	138	165

$X^2 = 12.41$, df $= 1$, p $< .001$
$\gamma = -.33$

TABLE 14

Satisfaction with Neighborhood by Wife's Age

| | | Satisfaction | | |
		Low	Medium	High
Wife's Age	39-under	39	47	114
	40-over	24	43	228

$$X^2 = 24.42, df = 2, p < .001$$
$$\gamma = .42$$

TABLE 15

Moving Intention by Husband's Age

| | | Moving Intention | |
		Move	Stay
Husband's Age	39-under	86	48
	40-over	73	167

$$X^2 = 40.10, df = 1, p < .001$$
$$\gamma = .61$$

TABLE 16

Moving Intention by Wife's Age

| | | Moving Intention | |
		Move	Stay
Wife's Age	39-under	113	87
	40-over	82	215

$$X^2 = 41.84, df = 1, p < .001$$
$$\gamma = .55$$

TABLE 17

Satisfaction with Neighborhood by Educational Level

		Satisfaction		
		Low	Medium	High
Educational Level*	Low (0-12)	51	60	219
	High (13-over)	10	29	123

$$X^2 = 8.98, df = 2, p < .02$$
$$\gamma = .25$$

* Mean school grade completed, husband and wife.

TABLE 18

Moving Intention by Educational Level

		Moving Intention	
		Move	Stay
Educational Level*	Low (0-6)	52	110
	Middle (7-12)	84	86
	High (13-over)	58	104

$$X^2 = 11.64, df = 2, p < .01$$

* Mean school grade completed, husband and wife.

TABLE 19

Satisfaction with Neighborhood by Occupation of
Head of Household

		Satisfaction	
		Low	Medium—High
Occupation of Head of Household *	High	30	269
	Low	33	158

$$X^2 = 5.46, df = 1, p < .05$$
$$\gamma = -.30$$

* "High" includes proprietors, professionals and semi-professionals, clerical and sales personnel and those living on investments. "Low" includes service, skilled, semi-skilled and unskilled workers, relief clients and the unemployed.

TABLE 20

Moving Intention by Occupation of Head of Household

| | | Moving Intention | |
		Move	Stay
	High	110	189
Occupation*	Middle	70	61
	Low	16	46

$$X^2 = 16.36, df = 2, p. < .001$$

* "Retired" omitted. "High" includes the same categories indicated in Table 15. "Middle" includes service, skilled, semi-skilled and unskilled workers. "Low" includes relief clients and the unemployed.

TABLE 21

Satisfaction with Neighborhood by Total Weekly Family Income

| | | Satisfaction | | |
		Low	Medium	High
Total Weekly	$120-over	8	27	125
Family Income	$40-$119	26	34	114
	$39-less	17	19	53

$$X^2 = 15.53, df = 4, p < .01$$
$$\gamma = -.28$$

TABLE 22

Moving Intention by Total Weekly Family Income

| | | Moving Intention | |
		Move	Stay
Total Weekly	$120-over	51	109
Family Income	$40-$119	95	79
	$39-less	31	60

$$X^2 = 20.45, df = 2, p < .001$$

TABLE 23

Satisfaction with Neighborhood by
Per Capita Weekly Income

| | | Satisfaction | | |
		Low	Medium	High
Per Capita Weekly Income	$40-over	7	22	99
	$20-$39	8	19	85
	$19-under	36	59	108

$$X^2 = 21.34, df = 4, p < .001$$
$$\gamma = -.33$$

TABLE 24

Moving Intention by Per Capita Weekly Income

| | | Moving Intention | |
		Move	Stay
Per Capita Weekly Income	$40-over	38	90
	$20-$39	46	66
	$19-under	93	92

$$X^2 = 13.21, df = 2, p < .01$$
$$\gamma = -.29$$

TABLE 25

Satisfaction with Neighborhood by Religious Affiliation

| | | Satisfaction | | |
		Low	Medium	High
Religious Affiliation*	Catholic	46	68	292
	Protestant	16	19	40

$$X^2 = 10.66, df = 2, p < .01$$

* Omits "other" and "none"

TABLE 26

Satisfaction with Neighborhood by Church Attendance

		Satisfaction		
		Low	Medium	High
Church Attendance	Regular	19	41	168
	Occasional or do not attend	43	49	173

$X^2 = 7.34$, df $= 2$, p $< .05$

$\gamma = -.21$

TABLE 27

Moving Intention by Church Attendance

		Moving Intention	
		Move	Stay
Church Attendance	Regular	71	157
	Occasional or do not attend	124	143

$X^2 = 12.06$, df $= 1$, p $< .001$

$\gamma = -.31$

TABLE 28

Satisfaction with Neighborhood by Quality of Housing

		Satisfaction		
		Low	Medium	High
Quality of Housing	High	6	17	108
	Middle	21	41	140
	Low	36	32	95

$X^2 = 27.73$, df $= 4$, p $< .001$

$\gamma = -.35$

TABLE 29

Moving Intention by Quality of Housing

		Moving Intention	
		Move	Stay
Quality of Housing	High	30	101
	Middle	91	111
	Low	75	90

$$X^2 = 20.18, df = 2, p < .001$$
$$\gamma = -.28$$

TABLE 30

Satisfaction with Neighborhood by Dwelling Type

		Satisfaction		
		Low	Medium	High
Dwelling Type	Single	21	53	170
	Multiple*	40	29	145

$$X^2 = 13.01, df = 2, p < .01$$

* Low-rent public housing omitted.

TABLE 31

Moving Intention by Dwelling Type

		Moving Intention	
		Move	Stay
Dwelling Type	Single	73	172
	Multiple*	113	102

$$X^2 = 24.63, df = 1, p < .001$$
$$\gamma = -.45$$

* Low rent public housing omitted.

TABLE 32

Moving Intention by Basis of Occupancy

| | | Moving Intention | |
		Move	Stay
Basis of Occupancy	Rent	154	118
	Own	42	184

$$X^2 = 74.81, df = 1, p < .001$$
$$\gamma = .70$$

TABLE 33

Moving Intention by Bedroom Density

| | | Moving Intention | |
		Move	Stay
Bedroom Density	1.50-under	88	195
	1.51-2.99	69	80
	3.00-over	39	27

$$X^2 = 21.88, df = 2 \; p < .001$$
$$\gamma = -.36$$

TABLE 34

Satisfaction with Neighborhood by Bedroom Density

| | | Satisfaction | | |
		Low	Medium	High
Bedroom Density	1.50-under	22	43	218
	1.51-2.99	20	30	98
	3.00-over	21	17	27

$$X^2 = 39.08, df = 4, p < .001$$
$$\gamma = -.40$$

TABLE 35

Satisfaction with Neighborhood by Improvements Index

| | | Satisfaction | | |
		Low	Medium	High
Improvements Index	0-14	41	35	62
	15-18	13	32	114
	19-over	9	23	167

$$X^2 = 71.67, df = 4, p < .001$$
$$\gamma = .54$$

TABLE 36

Moving Intention by Improvements Index

| | | Moving Intention | |
		Move	Stay
Improvements Index	0-14	72	67
	15-18	59	100
	19-over	65	135

$$X^2 = 13.29, df = 2, p < .01$$
$$\gamma = .25$$

TABLE 37

Satisfaction with Neighborhood by Homogeneity Index

| | | Satisfaction | |
		Low—Medium	High
Homogeneity Index	Homogeneous Neighborhood	58	179
	Heterogeneous Neighborhood	95	164

$$X^2 = 8.65, df = 1, p < .01$$
$$\gamma = -.28$$

TABLE 38

Moving Intention by Homogeneity Index

| | | Moving Intention | |
		Move	Stay
Homogeneity Index	Homogeneous Neighborhood	81	157
	Heterogeneous Neighborhood	115	145

$$X^2 = 5.41, df = 1, p < .05$$
$$\gamma = -.21$$

8 San Juan's Future

San Juan's Future

Let us try to summarize what we have learned about this seething metropolis, this ingenious device for converting field hands into mechanics and insurance salesmen, this crowded, colorful, squalid and luxurious city on a tropical beach.

We sought in vain for the symptoms of universal anomie and did not find them. The dominant note is one of satisfaction. More than two-thirds of our respondents have no complaint at all about the neighborhoods in which they live. Almost two-thirds hope to stay in their present homes indefinitely. The average San Juan family maintains active friendly relationships with more than half of its close neighbors and is on intimate terms with several. Neighbors have *not* been replaced by "nigh-dwellers." There is no indication that the migrant from the country receives less social support from those around than he was accustomed to in his village. Both the intensity and extensity of neighboring seem to increase as the migrant stays longer in the city and becomes more thoroughly acclimated. The urban world is a system in equilibrium for its inhabitants.

Mobility, too, shows a somewhat more favorable pattern than we might have expected from observation of changes in the visible surface of the city. The absolute rate of mobility is almost identical with that of the mainland.

Approximately twenty percent of the United States civilian population report a change of address[1] in any given year. This rate is exceeded in the Beach Front, the Central District and the Old Suburbs, but it exceeds the mobilities observed in the Old City, the Slum Belt and the New Suburbs of San Juan. Since the figures for San Juan are inflated by cyclical movement to and from New York, they represent quite moderate mobility. Furthermore, a very large proportion of all residential moves in San Juan are regarded as improvements by all concerned. In their study of social class and social change in Puerto Rico, Tumin and Feldman venture the large generalization that:

"There is very high morale in all segments of the Puerto Rican community. The present inequalities are not perceived as insuperable obstacles. The social order is viewed at all levels of the class structure as a fair and reasonable arrangement. Members of all classes feel well integrated and feel it is worth giving their loyalty to the society and their effort toward its development. In these terms, though they are decidedly unequally equipped with the required skills, people at all levels are relatively equally equipped for the future with the spirit required." [2]

They go on to say that Puerto Ricans feel far better off than the objective facts of income, education, and occupation would justify. We can say the same with respect to housing, neighborhood amenities, public services, and the entire urban environment. A tone of satisfaction permeates these interviews with regard to both the family's particular situation and the metropolitan community as a place to work and live.

The most salient finding of this study is that the intensity

[1] Nelson N. Foote, et al., *Housing Choices and Housing Constraints*, New York, McGraw-Hill, 1960, p. 134 et seq.
[2] Melvin M. Tumin with Arnold S. Feldman, *Social Class and Social Change in Puerto Rico*, Princeton, Princeton University Press, 1961, pp. 164-165.

of neighboring is correlated positively and significantly with every indicator of class position or social welfare. In San Juan, at least, the rich are better integrated into the urban network than the poor. Prosperity, *not* misery, likes company. Sociability declines as the need for support and assistance increases.[3]

The intensity of neighboring, it will be recalled, is correlated with occupational levels, the achieved education of both husband and wife, per capita income and total family income, housing quality, and duration of urban residence. Since all of these variables have been increasing steadily for this population as a whole, and for the overwhelming majority of individual families, there is no reason to suppose that neighboring will decrease or anomie will increase very sharply in San Juan in the foreseeable future.

Further indications that the San Juanero's satisfaction with urban life and his own corner of it is solidly grounded, are that residential satisfaction increases steadily with age, length of urban residence and duration of occupancy at a given address. Time weighs the scales towards improved satisfaction, just as anticipated by the hopeful ethos of this society.

The tangible development of the city provides additional confirmation for optimistic attitudes. The sheer volume of construction is unprecedented and impressive but in addition, the talent of local architects, and the opportunities for architectural display in tourist hotels, residences, and public buildings have given parts of the Beach Front and the New Suburbs a new elegance that can hardly be matched in the western hemisphere. Each passing month sees the improvement of more streets and the opening of new stretches of metropolitan highway. The renovation of the Old City, discussed for years, has finally been launched with sufficient momentum to continue. The steady improvement of public utilities, especially street lighting and telephone service, is a matter of daily observation. Extravagant local pride finds much to feed on and many a returning son sees San Juan as a handsomer, more exciting city than New York.

Finally, San Juan lacks many of the characteristic problems of North American cities of similar size because of its hybrid cultural history, and its strong tradition of public planning. Although problems of segregation by color and

---

[3] There are scattered bits of evidence to suggest that neighboring and socio-economic indicators are correlated in most other cultural settings also, but the evidence is not really sufficient to generalize.

ethnic origin exist in San Juan, they are much less severe
than in most North American cities. Although juvenile delinquency is widespread and getting worse, no part of San
Juan has the jungle atmosphere of the demoralized districts
of New York. Although much of the local housing is squalid
beyond belief, the homeless population is small and the
dispossessed stratum so conspicuous in most Latin American
capitals is absent.

It is interesting to note the incidence of problems listed
by Fisher in a careful account of the impact of decentraliza-
tion on North American cities. He writes that:

"As the central city loses its residential population, 'new suburban' cities spring up, forming an overexpanding megalopolis,
raising serious problems of representation, franchise, taxation,
planning and management." [4]

The first three of these problems are negligible in San
Juan and administrative devices for handling the latter two
are unusually well developed.

Given all of these favorable circumstances and trends, we
might be tempted to conclude that the long range planning
problems of San Juan are not serious or at least, that they
are certain to solve themselves in due course. Nothing could
be further from the truth. The problems that confront this
metropolis and its planning are severe, urgent and agoniz-
ingly difficult to solve.

They may be summarized under the following headings:

1. Urban sprawl
2. Traffic blight
3. The persistence of slums
4. The consequences of mass housing

All four of these problems are interrelated, of course, but
it may be instructive to consider them one by one, in the
flickering light of our data.

Urban Sprawl

San Juan has a more amorphous structure than almost any
other large city in the western world. The reasons for this

[4] Edward M. Fisher, "Changing Land Use in the Central City," *Stan-
ford Research Institute Journal*, Vol. 4, 4th quarter 1960.

will be recalled from the first chapter. The location of the Old City at the far end of a narrow island, surrounded by water and fortifications, disqualified it as a nucleus for metropolitan expansion, while its retention of many activities and installations prevented the development of a metropolitan nucleus in Santurce or Rio Piedras. This arrangement was viable, although awkward, as long as the metropolitan area was fairly compact. Under present conditions, with the center of population in the Old Suburbs, the absence of a central district is more severely felt. Aside from the strangulation of the metropolitan area by its traffic, which will be discussed separately, the lack of a center reduces the efficiency of almost every urban function—economic, administrative or cultural—and imparts a quality of inefficiency and wasted effort to the entire metropolitan system. It calls for endless duplication of facilities while depriving the city of many services to which its scale entitles it.

The Old City, isolated from its immediate hinterland, is stagnant, for all its busyness. Its museums, libraries, and theaters are underused, its shops and business establishments have little hope of future growth. The duplication of facilities means, besides an endless waste of time and travel, that metropolitan San Juan has no large-scale department stores or hospitals, no financial district, no entertainment center, no well-organized produce market, no fashion center, not even a convenient automobile row. Despite a tendency towards the development of a commercial nucleus around Stop 18 in Santurce, the overall pattern with respect to centralization is becoming worse, not better, as the facilities already duplicated in the Old City and the Central District are reproduced for the third time along the main avenues of the Old Suburbs.

Some other consequences of urban sprawl are more subtle, but no less serious. The new subdivisions with their standardized single family housing and their extraordinary isolation represent a way of life that scarcely belongs to the city, and many of their inhabitants have little opportunity for direct contact with city life. Although these vast housing tracts on the perimeter offer more comfort than the rural village or the city slum, their culture is in some ways poorer than either.

Traffic Blight

The problem of vehicular traffic is urgent in almost all modern cities; it is nearly overwhelming in San Juan. We know of no other city whose traffic jams are as severe and continuous, whose residential streets are so poorly protected from through traffic or whose suburbs are so poorly articulated to a transportation network. Few neighborhoods are safe from the intrusion of alien traffic; even fewer offer their residents convenient access to work, school, shopping and entertainment.

The problem is primarily due to the lack of a center, the duplication of facilities, and the urban sprawl already discussed. These factors maximize the distances to be covered in commuting, business operations, local deliveries, and every other routine activity. The problem is compounded by the still prevalent custom of taking lunch at home, which doubles the commuting burden, and by the local preference for large American cars that occupy maximum space in the traffic stream.

These are matters that cannot be easily changed. The preference for large American cars, for example, is plainly irrational on an island the size of Puerto Rico but since they are sold on more favorable terms than European cars and have vital functions as status symbols, a shift to smaller vehicles is unlikely. The custom of returning home for lunch is gradually being eroded but it fits too well with the local climate and family mores to be wholly abandoned. The lack of nucleation, as we have seen, is a fundamental feature of the ecological pattern.

Given these obstacles, there is no reason to suppose that traffic blight in San Juan will be easily cured but all the more reason for urging that it not be neglected and that the planning of freeways, street improvements, and public transportation, be guided by long range strategies for reducing congestion rather than the self-defeating goal of increasing the vehicular capacity of already congested routes.

The Persistence of Slums

The level of living in the Slum Belt is too low to be tolerated by a metropolitan community committed to economic and social self-improvement. As this study has shown, the slum dwellers, too, find their conditions abominable. The noise, smells, dirt, dampness and insalubrity, the difficulty of access, the absence or inadequacy of public utilities, the fantastic crowding, and the threat of dangerous and demoralized neighbors, combine to make the slums very unpleasant indeed. It will come as a shock to many Puerto Ricans who have watched their government's gigantic efforts at slum clearance in recent years to realize that, although the growth of the Slum Belt has been checked, only trifling progress has been made towards its removal. The decline of the slum population has recently averaged less than one-half of one percent per year—a rate that, if continued, would give the Slum Belt two centuries more of existence.

Meanwhile a new generation of slums can be seen emerging here and there in the Central District and—more significantly—in some of the more hastily constructed subdivisions in the New Suburbs where a combination of physicial deterioration, inaccessibility, and limited public services, may soon produce conditions that resemble the slums along the sewage canal in every feature but the smell.

The Consequences of Mass Housing

The San Juan Urban Area has taken greater advantage of Federal low rent housing programs than any mainland city. Its public projects have been proportionately larger and more ambitious than those of any other community. As Back's study[5] and some of our own findings show, this program has been moderately successful, whether evaluated in terms of

[5] *Op. cit.*

city planning or through the eyes of the people concerned. Yet, there is a striking contrast between the ambivalent acceptance of low-rent public housing, and the wild enthusiasm for small jerry-built subdivision houses on the remote outskirts. The reasons for this difference appear plainly in our data on residential satisfaction. In his housing preferences, the San Juanero belongs entirely to North America, not to Latin America or Europe. His preference for single family housing over multiple dwellings is overwhelming and cannot be satisfied by row housing or low-rise apartments. The free standing family house on its own landscaped plot of ground, however small, is the only type of housing that has emotional value for the average San Juan family.

Home ownership is both a sentimental symbol, and a mode of satisfaction. The fact of ownership is what counts, not the details of the transaction. The home owner's equity in his property may be negligible, his tenure less secure than that of a renter with a lease, his house identical with those of his neighbors and his freedom abridged by project rules that forbid him to make any decorative changes. Nevertheless, in Puerto Rico—and the United States as well—home ownership is the goal of most renting families and once achieved, it is highly valued.

Although low-rent public projects have preoccupied planners in San Juan far more than low cost private projects, the future seems to belong to the latter form. The proportion of the population housed in single family suburban subdivisions is already much greater than the population in low rent multiple apartments and growing much faster. It is increasingly plain that more public interest and more planning effort needs to be focused on private developments. The future shape of the city is already setting in a mold whose advantages and disadvantages have not been carefully considered.

Segregation

The traditional Spanish city encouraged a much greater mixture of land use than a North American city and this accounts for much of its charm and amenity. After half a century of blind and mechanical zoning, the importance of local diversity and the advantages of mixed land use in the city are just beginning to be seen and preached by city planners and city lovers in the United States.

San Juan has been happily free of the bitter dilemmas of racial and ethnic segregation but it is not immune from such tendencies. The neighborhood data show a tendency towards informal discrimination against non-whites and non-Catholics. The arrangement of the new suburban enclaves tends to reinforce these latent tendencies to segregation.

Once again, what is needed is not a new master plan but a shift of emphasis. "Good" residential districts with all individual initiative and diversity zoned out of them, are thoroughly bad for a living city.

Envoi

Nothing in our survey justifies pessimism about San Juan or its future. The rural migrants who throng into this great city and others like it may see their own advantage more clearly than the critics who urge them to stay at home and enjoy the blessings of a simple and superstitious village society.

In any event, neither the sociologist nor the planner has any choice about the great phenomenon of urbanization. The villagers continue to swell the populations of great cities and will probably do so as long as our civilization—a name given to the life of cities—persists. The present study has shown, like many others, that the typical city neighborhood is a viable, well-integrated social system, capable of meeting the needs of its inhabitants rather successfully and facilitating a painless adjustment to the urban environment. The skillful and sensitive planner will not want to substitute some symmetrical scheme for the living network that constitutes a city, but its very complexity and want of symmetry will urge him perpetually to improve it.

Appendix

The Interview Schedule

The Interview Schedule (Translated)

University of Puerto Rico   Social Science Research Center
College of Social Science
Urban Sociology Project   Interview Phase

Date:_____ Hour:_____ Duration:_____
Color: White:___ Light Mulatto:___ Dark Mulatto:___ Negro:___
Unit Number:_____ Interview Number:_____
Address:_____ Years at present address:_____
Marital Status: Single____ Married____ Divorced____ Widow____
          Separated____
Number in Family:_____ Age of wife:_____ Age of husband:_____
  Ages of children:___, ___, ___ Others, ages and relationship:_____
Education of wife:_____ Education of husband:_____
Birthplace of wife:_____ First address in San Juan:_____
          Previous address:_____
Birthplace of husband:_____ First address in San Juan:_____
          Previous address:_____
Occupation of all members of the family who are working and their
  weekly salary:_____

_____

Other income (source and amount):_____
Total family income last week:_____
Means of transportation to work by principal breadwinner:_____
  Convenience of transportation to work:_____
Means of transportation of oldest child to school:_____
  Convenience of transportation to school:_____
Housing unit type:_____ Socio-economic level:_____
Number of bedrooms:___ Bathroom: Private___ Shared___ None___
Monthly rent:_____ Type of occupancy:_____
Church membership:_____ Attendance: (previous month)___
Other membership:_____ Attendance:_____
Other membership:_____ Attendance:_____
Other membership:_____ Attendance:_____

Unit Number	Neighborhood Scale							
	0	1	2	3	4	5	6	Y
1. ————————	—	—	—	—	—	—	—	—
2. ————————	—	—	—	—	—	—	—	—
3. ————————	—	—	—	—	—	—	—	—
4. ————————	—	—	—	—	—	—	—	—
5. ————————	—	—	—	—	—	—	—	—
6. ————————	—	—	—	—	—	—	—	—
7. ————————	—	—	—	—	—	—	—	—
8. ————————	—	—	—	—	—	—	—	—
9. ————————	—	—	—	—	—	—	—	—
10. ————————	—	—	—	—	—	—	—	—
11. ————————	—	—	—	—	—	—	—	—
12. ————————	—	—	—	—	—	—	—	—
13. ————————	—	—	—	—	—	—	—	—
14. ————————	—	—	—	—	—	—	—	—
15. ————————	—	—	—	—	—	—	—	—
16. ————————	—	—	—	—	—	—	—	—
17. ————————	—	—	—	—	—	—	—	—
18. ————————	—	—	—	—	—	—	—	—
19. ————————	—	—	—	—	—	—	—	—
20. ————————	—	—	—	—	—	—	—	—

(Draw a circle around the number of the unit you are interviewing.)

Final questions in relation to neighbors.

27. Who are your three best friends among your neighbors?
    (Indicate the number of the unit if on the map)
    a._____ b._____ c._____

28. Which three of your relatives have you seen most frequently dur-
    ing the last month? What is your relation to each person? How
    frequently have you seen each person during the last month?

Name	Address	Relation	Scale Value

29. Do you work outside your home? (If yes, continue; if no, go on to
    the following series) Yes_____ No_____

30. Who are your three closest associates at work? How frequently do
    you lunch together with each of these persons? Do you drink coffee
    or go to any work related activities together? What position does
    that person have at your place of employment?

Name	Address	Relation	Scale Value

31. Of those persons with whom you go out and visit, etc., who are
    the three you have seen most frequently during the last month?
    Aside from being your friends, do you have any other relationship
    with them? (Relatives, work associates, etc.) How frequently have
    you visited them during the last month?

Name	Address	Relation	Scale Value

32. Do you have any relatives or neighbors working in the same place
    where you work? Yes_____ No_____

33. Now I would like to ask you about your relationship to your hus-
    band's relatives, work associates, and recreational friends.
    Of your husband's relatives which three has he seen most often
    during the last month? What relationship are they to him? How
    often have you seen them?

Name	Address	Relation	Scale Value

34. Would you be able to tell me which three persons are your husband's closest work associates? What positions do these persons
have at his place of employment? How often have you seen each
of them during the last month?

Name	Address	Relation	Scale Value

35. Are your husband's three closest recreational friends the same ones
as yours? Yes_____ No_____ Some_____
(If "no" or "some" continue to next question.)

36. Of your husband's recreational friends, which three has he seen
most often during the last month?

Name	Address	Scale Value

37. Do you believe that this neighborhood is a good place to live? Why
or why not?_____

38. Do you intend to stay here permanently? Yes_____ No_____
If not, to what part of the city do you intend to move?_____

Index

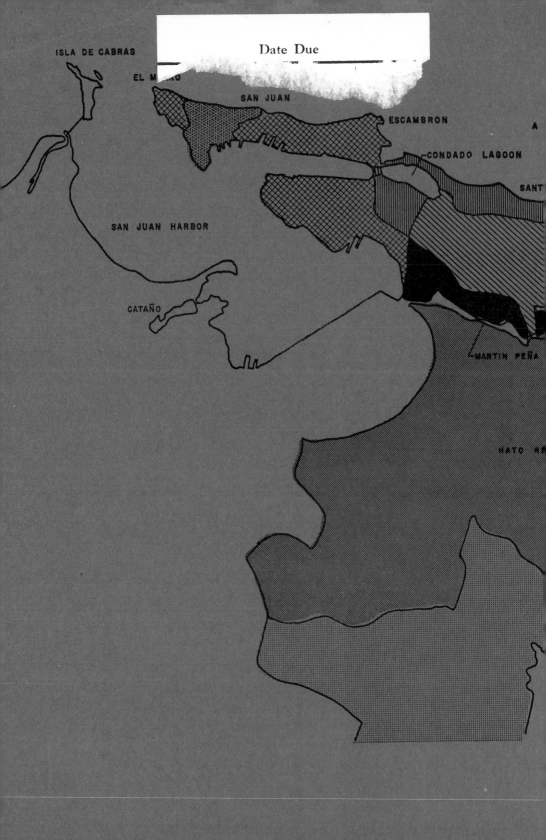

ISLA DE CABRAS

EL M___O

Date Due

SAN JUAN

ESCAMBRON

A

CONDADO LAGOON

SANT

SAN JUAN HARBOR

CATAÑO

MARTIN PEÑA

HATO R___